BUSINESS ISSUES, COMPETITION AND ENTREPRENEURSHIP

POST-INVESTMENT MONITORING

INTERCULTURAL SYNERGY VALUATION

BUSINESS ISSUES, COMPETITION AND ENTREPRENEURSHIP

Additional books and ebooks in this series can be found on Nova's website under the Series tab.

BUSINESS ISSUES, COMPETITION AND ENTREPRENEURSHIP

POST-INVESTMENT MONITORING

INTERCULTURAL SYNERGY VALUATION

LIVIU WARTER

nova
science publishers
New York

Library of Congress Cataloging-in-Publication Data

Names: Warter, Liviu, author.
Title: Post-investment monitoring : intercultural synergy valuation / Liviu Warter.
Description: New York : Nova Science Publishers, Inc., [2019] | Series: Business issues, competition and entrepreneurship | Includes bibliographical references and index.
Identifiers: LCCN 2019030823 (print) | LCCN 2019030824 (ebook) | ISBN 9781536159592 (hardcover) | ISBN 9781536159608 (adobe pdf)
Subjects: LCSH: Consolidation and merger of corporations. | Business enterprises--Purchasing. | Corporate culture.
Classification: LCC HD2746.5 .W37 2019 (print) | LCC HD2746.5 (ebook) | DDC 658.1/62--dc23
LC record available at https://lccn.loc.gov/2019030823
LC ebook record available at https://lccn.loc.gov/2019030824

Published by Nova Science Publishers, Inc. † New York

*This book is dedicated to my late parents, Sarina and Erich,
and to my brother Iulian with love and gratitude*

CONTENTS

PREFACE

This book is focused on post-investment issues, particularly on intercultural synergy, and M&A performance. The most challenging part of the M&A process is the integration of two entities that present different organizational and national cultures.

Post-merger integration phase is a complex operation of mixing and repositioning processes to reify synergies that typically stimulate mergers and acquisitions. Intercultural synergy is the mixture of diverse cultural elements like traditions, values, norms, practices, behaviours etc. in such a way that the result is a construction of higher value than the sum of elements.

This book exerts to find an explanation for M&A performance in terms of the impact that cultural differences have on the post-merger integration process. It emphasises the role of post-investment monitoring and intercultural synergies achievement.

The almost general opinion is that cultural influences are important in M&A. Despite this, the outcomes of this study reveal the underestimation of the role of cultural integration in M&A literature.

This monograph is seeking to deepen the apprehension of the impact of cultural differences on M&A performance. Regardless of the increased attention directed at the implications of cultural differences for the M&A performance the outcomes are still doubtful.

The concept of "intercultural synergy" is still poorly understood despite a growing body of research on synergy creation. Generically, there is an inadequate practical approach although most scholars highlight the importance of intercultural synergy in M&A.

The main goal of this book was to uncover intercultural issues that managers encountered during the post-investment phase and they should have discovered during the pre-investment phase. Intercultural synergy has a strong impact on M&A. Both national and organizational cultures are determinants for maximizing the intercultural synergy.

A quantitative descriptive approach was employed in this study. Based on Factor Analysis, a number of 19 factors were extracted structured in 9 dimensions. They all start from 77 basic items. General linear model was used in some of the cases because the analyses include both numeric (interval level) and categorical variables (nominal level). The other dependencies were studied using statistical regression.

The focal point of this book was to check whether there is a significant relationship between the M&A outcomes, synergy and the cultural differences. It examined also the relationship between the perception on the M&A integration process and outcome and the cultural specificity.

The use of regression and General Linear Model analyses assisted the statistical aims of the research by pointing out a positive considerable relationship.

Generally, the analysis results indicated a considerable relationship between the M&A outcomes, synergy and the cultural differences. The same can be said about the relationship between the perception on the M&A integration process and outcome and the cultural specificity.

This book might offer support for the interaction between cultural specificity and the post-M&A stage, as the cultural variables impact the perceptions on M&A outcomes, M&A integration and intercultural synergy creation. This study expands the current paradigm of post-M&A activities to include the study of cultural issues by grouping them in factors and dimensions. The main theories have been almost exclusively developed not by taking into consideration the concept of intercultural synergy, as it is in the current monograph. Yet, professionals worldwide face with the assignment of comprehending and examining M&A cultural issues across professional diversity.

This book integrates the research on national, organizational and professional culture, into a theory of M&A performance and outcome. It investigates not only the outcomes and intercultural synergy but also the perception on these issues.

In the area of intercultural management, this book reveals that the Culture Clusters is a very helpful and strong tool. It appears that national culture might influence perceptions on M&A in some culture clusters much more than in others.

List of Abbreviations

m	Management
cvp	Company values and practices
f	Finance
p	Production
hrm	Human resource management
dcg	Contains few different cultural groups
vcd	Low level of valuing cultural differences
tcd	Low tolerance of cultural differences
u	Uniculturalism
boc	Very strong belief in own competitiveness
i	Strong identity
sbt	Strong sense of belonging together
rc	No readiness for change
f	Low level of flexibility
c	Low level of creativity
uaf	Uncertainty about the future
go	Divergent goals and objectives
ci	Poor coordination/integration
pt	Low professional trust
mrs	Mistrust in rewards system
mao	Mistrust in advancement opportunities

c	Poor communication
lkp	Loss of key persons
m	Lack of motivation
il	Poor integration leadership
oi	Low organizational identification
is	Low intercultural synergy
a	Increase in absenteeism
rc	Resistance to change
s	Sabotage
mu	Misunderstandings
mt	Mistrust
irpw	Incapacity to reconcile different points of view
urpw	Unwillingness to reconcile different points of view
c	Conflicts
cdu	Cultural differences understanding
m	Multilingualism
adc	Adaptation to a different culture
aoc	Awareness of own culture
ro	Respect for otherness
ca	Communicative awareness
bf	Behavioral flexibility
rc	Readiness for change

Chapter 1

INTRODUCTION

1.1. THE MERGERS AND ACQUISITIONS PHENOMENON

This book focuses on post-investment aspects especially on intercultural synergy, and M&A performance.

Successful corporate acquirers continued focusing on valuation, due diligence, and integration, to reach strategic aims and increase shareholder value. The most challenging part of the process is the integration of two different firms that feature different organizational and national cultures. The contradictory findings suggest the relationship between culture, post-merger integration processes, and M&A performance to be rather complex and require further empirical studies.

The relationship between cultural differences and M&A outcomes is more complicated than previously regarded. Scholars and practitioners should focus on how cultural differences affect M&A performance.

Mergers and Acquisitions are instruments to reach particular strategic and deal objectives by combining two companies. M&A is a common short expression for mergers and acquisitions, grouping the two notions as a single domain of interest.

The notion Merger can be defined as the legal consolidation of two equal corporations, in which one corporation or both are losing their entity.

Mergers ordinarily require the endorsement of the acquiring and target company's shareholders.

Acquisition implies that one company purchases 100% of the shares and thereby, takes over the possession of the acquired asset. The deals can be through share deals by acquiring the shares of the target company or by asset deals meaning buy of property holdings.

Whether some compounds are structured as a merger or acquisition is dependent on not only on the underlying deal, but also on other legal, taxation and psychological implications. An acquisition may or may not lead to a merger, from a strategic and investment banking point of view the two concepts require a similar expertise and procedure.

Cross-border M&A are a principal means, by which companies can evolve and internationalize in foreign markets.

Foreign direct investment (FDI) can be defined as an investment involving a long-term association and reflecting an enduring interest and control of a resident entity in one economy (foreign direct investor or parent enterprise) in an enterprise resident in an economy other than that of the foreign direct investor (FDI enterprise or affiliate enterprise or foreign affiliate). FDI may be carried on by individuals as well as business entities.

Integration phase is the last stage of M&A in which the strategic and value-creating aims have to be realized by the integration of the acquired company.

Post-merger integration phase is a complex process of mixing and repositioning processes to materialize possible efficiencies and synergies that typically motivate mergers and acquisitions.

Three distinct ways in order to best measure post M&A performance are acknowledged: synergy achievement, absolute performance, and lastly relative performance.

Intercultural synergy is the mixture of cultural diverse elements like traditions, values, norms, practices, behaviors etc. in such a way, that a structure results which is of higher value than the sum of elements.

1.2. Recent Evolutions in Mergers and Acquisition

Powered by a resurgence of deals over $5 billion, the value of worldwide M&A totaled US$3.5 trillion during full year 2014, a 47% increase from comparable 2013 levels and the strongest annual period for worldwide deal making since 2007. Ninety-five deals with a value greater than $5 billion were announced during full year 2014, more than double the value and number of large-cap deals announced during 2013. Just over 40,400 worldwide deals were announced during full year 2014, a 6% increase compared to last year.

M&A activity for European targets totaled US$869.8 billion during full year 2014, an increase of 55% compared to the level of activity seen during full year 2013. With US$716.2 billion in announced deals during full year 2014, Asia Pacific M&A registered the strongest annual period for deal making in the region since records began in 1980.

Cross-border M&A activity totaled US$1.3 trillion during full year 2014, accounting for 37% of overall M&A volume and a 78% increase over full year 2013 levels. Cross border M&A accounted for 31% of total M&A activity during full year 2013 (Thomson Reuters, n.d.).

Primack (2015) referred to large deals in 2014 — 95 valued at $5 billion or more — were a key driver, given that the overall number of global M&A transactions only climbed by 6%. This includes the year's three largest announced deals: Comcast Corp.'s $70.67 billion deal for Time Warner Cable, AT&T's $67 billion purchase of DirecTV and Activis paying $66 billion for Allergan.

Ten of the year's 15 largest acquisitions were for companies based in the United States, where volume climbed by 51.4% to $1.53 trillion. European M&A 55%, while Asia-Pacific hit its largest-ever total at $716 billion. Geographic regions with year-over-year decreases included Eastern Europe (-53.5%), Central America (-30.1%) and the Africa/Middle East (-16.9%). The largest large country increase was for France (up 239% to $165 billion), while Germany was on the flipside (-21.6% to $73 billion).

Cross-border M&A has been one of the key features of 2015. In 2015 $1.07 trillion in cross-border deals have been announced and this includes three of the ten largest deals in 2015. Europe has been at the centre of cross-border M&A, with European companies participating in 53% of all announced deals. The North America-Europe deal corridor has dominated, worth $311 billion. US companies have led the way, having announced $114 billion worth of M&As in Europe, of which $44 billion are in the UK. The growth markets nations have announced $49.6 billion of acquisitions in G7 nations, whereas the G7 nations have announced only $30.7 billion in M&A deals in growth markets, the lowest in over a decade. Cross-border deal flow is expected to be a key theme in the coming years, as major economies strike agreements and alliances to bolster trade. For instance the recently agreed Trans-Pacific Partnership between 12 Pacific-Rim countries, including the US, Japan, Canada and Australia, is the biggest global trade agreement in two decades (Deloitte, n.d.).

In their study, Ernst & Young (n.d.) observes that as companies increasingly acquire digital assets with different cultural and operational models, integration becomes even more challenging. The need to retain acquired talent and expertise is paramount. Integration considerations have long needed to be part of the front-end deal strategy – now more than ever in an increasingly digital world.

Driven by deal making over $5 billion, America's volume increased 51% over totals reached last year, accruing US$2.1 trillion in activity from 15,734 announced deals. US targeted M&A also posted significant gains, rising 51.5% over announced M&A in 2013. US-targeted volume accrued a total of US$1.5 trillion in 2014, driven by 9,814 deals.

Accumulating US$204 billion in transaction value, announced Canadian Involvement activity rose by 38.6% over the totals reached in 2013. Completed Canadian Involvement also rose, to US$188.6 billion from 1,962 deals, a 26.5% increase from completed activity in 2013. (Thomson Reuters, n.d.)

Several US M&A records were shattered in 2015. The desire to do deals remains strong and the financing to execute them is in place for 2016. While appetites remain high, executives will continue to exert patience and walk away from deals with too many risk factors. Companies will seek opportunities outside of their industry sector in the search for new growth and innovation. Given the unrelenting power of disruptive forces impacting almost every industry – whether it is through changing consumer preferences or the introduction of new technologies – companies sitting on the side lines will do so at their own peril. Markets will remain supportive of companies seeking inorganic growth opportunities (Ernst & Young, 2015).

In a reflection on such demands, Deloitte (n.d.) points to the fact that companies often underestimate both the complexity and true cost of integration. Based on Deloitte's experience of delivering post- merger integration projects, the total cost of integration represents, on average, 5% of the deal value.

Some of the most important U.S. deals announced in 2015 are (Street Insider, n.d.):

- $37B Aetna - Humana
- $37B Avago Tech - Broadcom
- $32.6B Energy Transfer Equity - Williams Companies
- $28.3B ACE - Chubb Corp.
- $21B AbbVie - Pharmacyclics

Announced M&A activity with Asian involvement reached a record high, grossing US$743.9 billion from 10,416 deals, respectively, a 62% increase over the US$459.5 billion recorded in 2013. China remained the most targeted nation in the region, with US$390.4 billion of value from 4,520 deals. Companies in the financial sector were the most targeted, with US$142.4 billion accumulated from 1,201 deals. The top deal in the region was CITIC Pacific's acquisition of the main assets of its state-owned parent, CITIC Group, valued at US$42.2 billion, which surpassed the previous record-holding deal in the Asia Pacific (excluding Japan) region - PCCW's US$35.5 billion acquisition of Cable & Wireless HKT in 2000.

Asian buy-side financial sponsor M&A activity accumulated US$77.8 billion in value driven by 14 deals valued over US$1 billion (compared to 4 deals in 2013). The top deal was Sinopec's US$17.5 billion retail stake sale to 25 domestic and foreign investors. (Thomson Reuters, n.d.)

Outbound M&A activities from Asia Pacific in 2015 registered a year's total of US$313.4 billion on the back of 1,268 deals. China, Japan, Hong Kong, Australia and Singapore are the top 5 most active acquirers in 2015 by deal volume among Asia Pacific countries.

Inbound deals into Asia Pacific totaled US$210.1 billion for 2015. Intra-regional deals within Asia Pacific accounted for 60% of the region's inbound deals (by value) for the full year.

2016 outlook for cross-border M&A remains positive, as a number of ASEAN countries undergo regulatory reforms to attract foreign investments, and India is likely to remain a hot target.

The value of inbound deals into Asia Pacific by Western buyers and others outside the region reached US$83.4 billion in 2015, up 2% from 2014. India and Australia emerged as the favored targets by US and European companies, while China continues to be the most targeted country overall with 254 deals worth US$42.3 billion in 2015. India's technology sector was particularly attractive to foreign buyers last year, rising to 44 deals, including transactions such as US-based IT outsourcing firm Virtusa's acquisition of a 53% stake in India software company Polaris for US$350 million.

Transactional activity in the Asia Pacific region will continue to rise from 2016 to 2018 on the back of the region's strong economic fundamentals, with M&A activity in Asia Pacific peaking at US$755 billion in 2018. Myanmar, Vietnam and the Philippines are also likely to draw more interest from foreign buyers in 2016 as their domestic markets continue to develop. More China-related M&A deals are also on the horizon, with China's currency becoming more widely used in trade and finance as the liberalization process continues. Technology is likely to remain a hot sector for cross-border M&A activity, be it for China because of government policy, or for India because of the country's strong culture of innovation, growing educated middle class, and the proliferation of IT outsourcing companies.

A detailed study, CMS Legal Services (n.d.) remarks that this was not a great time to be a dealmaker in Emerging Europe. While investment bankers and M&A lawyers in other parts of the world enjoyed a well-earned rest this Christmas after their busiest year since 2007, their peers in Central and Eastern Europe were nervously following the free fall of the rouble. Merger and acquisition activity in Emerging Europe in 2014 saw a whopping 43% drop in deal values, falling from €112 billion in 2013 to €64 billion in 2014. The number of announced deals with a value above €1 million recorded a 14% annual decline to a total of 2,198 transactions. M&A in Russia accounted for 33% of all deals in Emerging Europe and 47% of the total deal value in 2014. Poland came second with a 13% share in deal numbers, closely followed by Turkey with 12% (CMS Legal Services, n.d.).

In 2015 economic circumstances improved and financial conditions stabilized thanks to intervention by the European Central Bank, though not necessarily to the same level in every European country. The level of divestments by Spanish MNEs, for example, declined markedly; furthermore they were especially active in the first half of 2015, completing some large acquisitions such as: Repsol SA's purchase of Talisman Energy Inc (Canada) for US$8.3 billion and Banco de Sabadell SA's acquisition of TSB Banking Group Plc (UK) for US$2.5 billion.

The European M&A market was booming with the total value of transactions exceeding the pre-crisis highs reached in 2007-2008. And this in defiance of the volatility in the world's equity markets. This M&A boom, also, masks a decrease in the number of transactions being agreed. Cash-rich corporates considered deals in Europe due to the low prices, a significant driver of increased M&A activity. The UK was the most frequently targeted Western European country, with 7,260 deals worth a collective USD 548,699 million in 2015.

Five of the top Europe Deals (in million USD) in 2015 are (FactSet, n.d.):

- SABMiller Plc - Anheuser-Busch InBev SA
  €106,904.9 Consumer Non-Durables
- BG Group Plc - Royal Dutch Shell €74,719.0 Energy Minerals
- Allergan Plc (Generic Drugs Operations) - Teva Pharmaceuticals Industries Ltd. €36,934.1 Health Technology

- Perrigo Co. - Mylan NV €33,551.5 Health Technology
- Baxalta, Inc. - Shire Plc €28,167.2 Health Technology

The CSE region has reportedly seen a 3.0 percent growth in its mergers and acquisitions sector. US investors have been the most active in the region, followed by Great Britain Germany, and Austria. Seemingly most of the interest went towards the IT sector, while, the biggest transactions took place in the banking sector.

Roberts (2015) mentioned the top 10 M&A deals of 2014, ranked by transaction value (in million USD). Below are some of them:

- CITIC Pacific's acquisition of CITIC Ltd (100% - 42,247.5)
- Holcim Ltd's acquisition of Lafarge SA (100% - 39,544.6)
- Haliburton Co's acquisition of Baker Hughes Inc (100% - 38,477.9)
- Some of the biggest M&A deals of 2015 are listed below:
- Pfizer and Allergan: $191 billion
- Shell and BG Group: $81 billion
- Charter and Time Warner Cable: $78 billion

As concerns failed M&A transactions, Golman (2014) wrote about the five largest failed deals in 2014. Two of them are presented below.

One of these failed deals is T-Mobile US/Iliad SA: Following a four month pursuit of T-Mobile US, Iliad SA, a French telecommunications company, abandoned its attempt at consolidation and entry into the North American market. After a weak initial offering in July, Iliad stocks slid 25% and concern grew as to whether or not the company had the financial resources to follow through with the deal. Even a follow-up offer several months later failed to capture the interest of Deutsche Telekom, T-Mobile's majority owner, leaving the deal dead in its tracks.

Another one is Omnicom/PublicisGroupe: The $35 billion merger between Omnicom and PublicisGroupe SA was called off by both parties in May after reports of disagreements between executives over the leadership of the combined entity, and which company would legally be acquiring the other. In the end, the ability to house the world's most prominent advertising agencies under one roof wasn't worth the endless clashing of corporate cultures.

An article by Porzio (2016) examines the trends in 2016 for M&As. He believes that M&A in 2016 will be influenced by the following four trends:

- Due to greater technology, social deal making will take a leap forward and will help change the way deals get done
- Fewer deals will leak
- Companies will manage shareholder activism by getting closer to their largest shareholders
- Antitrust – more pressure, more scrutiny

According to Thomson Reuters (2017), worldwide M&A activity totaled US$3.7 trillion during full year 2016, a 16% decrease from full year 2015 levels and third largest annual period for worldwide deal making since records began in 1980. Just over 100 deals with a value greater than $5 billion were announced during full year 2016, their combined value down 30% compared to a year before. Overall, 46,055 worldwide deals were announced during full year 2016, a 1% increase compared to last year.

M&A activity for United States targets totaled US$1.7 trillion during full year 2016, a decrease of 17% compared to the level of activity seen during 2015. With US$896.3 billion in announced deals during the full year 2016, Asia Pacific M&A fell 22% compared to a year before. Asia Pacific targets accounted for 25% of worldwide M&A, compared to 21% for Europe.

Bureau Van Dijk (2017) also reveals that both the volume and value of global mergers and acquisitions (M&A) declined in 2016 after a record breaking year on both fronts in 2015, according to information collected by the leading M&A database Zephyr. In all there were 96,665 deals worth a combined USD 4,734,165 million announced over the course of the 12 months. Value declined 21 per cent on 2015, when deal making of USD 6,011,581 million was announced, while volume fell 10 per cent from 107,182 over the same timeframe. Both volume and value were also surpassed by the 102,176 deals worth USD 4,802,023 million announced in

2014. However, despite the relatively disappointing showing when compared with 2014 and 2015, the latter of which was a record-breaking year, 2016's value is still significantly higher than any other year since the previous record deal levels of 2007.

Thomson Reuters (2017) highlights that Americas M&A volume during 2016 decreased 12.8% from comparable 2015 levels, accruing US$2.2 trillion in activity from 17,146 announced deals.

US Targeted M&A also saw a decrease, down 16.8% compared to announced M&A during 2015. US-targeted volume accrued a total of US$1.7 trillion during 2016 from 11,061 deals. Announced M&A activity with EMEA involvement totaled US$1.3 trillion from 18,772 deals in 2016, down 8.7% compared to the US$1.4 trillion reached in 2015.

Announced M&A volume with Asian involvement for full year 2016 decreased by 8% compared to the same period in 2015, accruing US$1.1 trillion in value from 13,363 deals, the highest number of deals on record. Meanwhile, 7,768 deals were completed this year valued at US$745.8 billion, down 9.9% in value from the same period last year. The top announced Asian-involvement deal for 2016 was the US$46.6 billion acquisition of Syngenta, a Swiss biotech, by CNAC Saturn, a subsidiary of China state-owned China National Chemical. The biggest deal from the fourth quarter of 2016 in Asia, was the acquisition of India's Essar Oil for US$12.9 billion by Petrol Complex (a subsidiary of PJSC Rosneft Oil).

Japanese M&A volume for full year 2016 registered a 1.5% decrease from comparable 2015 levels, accruing US$192.1 billion in activity, the third strongest full year period for Japanese M&A on record after 1999's US$242.4 billion and 2015's US$194.9 billion. 3,394 Japanese involvement deals were announced in 2016 -149 deals more than were announced in 2015, marking the highest deal count on record.

Bureau Van Dijk (2017) underlines that despite the decline in value recorded in 2016, there have still been a number of "mega" deals announced over the course of year; in all there were 35 transactions worth USD 10,000 million or more announced in 2016. The most valuable deal to have been announced over the 12 months was worth USD 124,444 million as Anheuser-Busch InBev acquired beer manufacturer SABMiller via its

Newbelco acquisition vehicle. Second place was taken by AT&T's USD 108,700 million purchase of US media and entertainment conglomerate Time Warner, which was announced in October and is expected to close by the end of 2017. As such, although aggregate value declined in 2016 dealmakers are still clearly willing to pay high prices to get the companies they want, but a decline in volume after a record-breaking year in 2015 appears to have held value down over the 12 months.

Analyzing the year 2017, Bureau Van Dijk (2018) mentions that the volume and value of global mergers and acquisitions (M&A) declined. In all, there were 96,082 deals worth a combined USD 4,740,969 million announced over the course of the 12 months. In terms of volume, this represented an 8 per cent drop on the 104,559 deals announced in 2016, while value slipped 3 per cent from USD 4,892,779 million over the same timeframe. The result is particularly disappointing as it represented the second consecutive annual decline in both volume and value (2015: 109,615 deals worth USD 5,871,017 million). However, the result represents an improvement on 2012 and 2013.

In the same vein, Thomson Reuters (2018) shows that M&A activity totaled US$3.6 trillion during full year 2017, on par with full year 2016 levels and the fourth consecutive year to surpass $3 trillion. Deals with a value less than US$1 billion totaled US$1.3 trillion, up 7% compared to full year 2016. By number, deals less than US$1 billion also increased 7% compared to a year ago. Overall, 49,448 worldwide deals were announced during 2017, an increase of 3% compared to a year ago and the strongest year for M&A, by number of deals, since records began in 1980.

Bureau Van Dijk (2018) emphasizes that several world regions actually attracted more value in 2017 than in 2016. Examples include Western Europe, where value climbed 6 per cent from USD 1,213,785 million to USD 1,281,917 million over the 12 months, as well as the Far East and Central Asia (USD 1,250,128 million to USD 1,275,161 million).

Once again, the US attracted the most investment in 2017, and also topped the country rankings by volume. Companies based in the country were targeted in 20,897 deals worth a combined USD 1,455,399 million. Its nearest rival on both fronts was China, which placed second with 13,679 deals worth USD 720,892 million. The UK was third, with 5,832 deals totaling USD 285,419 million. The US's position at the head of the country rankings is unsurprising given that it featured in nine of the year's top 20 deals by value, including all of the top three. The largest of all featured an insurance player as CVS Health agreed to pick up Aetna for USD 77,000 million. This was followed by the Walt Disney Company's USD 66,100 million takeover of Twenty-First Century Fox, which was announced in December, while third place was taken by British American Tobacco's USD 49,400 million acquisition of Reynolds American. The largest deal with a non-US target involved Germany-based Linde, which Praxair agreed to acquire for USD 37,861 million in June. The buyer intends to carry out the deal via a newly-formed entity known as Linde plc. Germany actually placed fourth on the country rankings by value in 2017 (USD 175,240 million), of which 22 per cent is attributable to the Linde deal.

The value of M&A targeting companies based in Western Europe in 2017 was the second-highest recorded since the global financial crisis of 2007-08 as total deal making rose 6 per cent year-on-year to USD 1,281,917 million on the back of 13 deals each worth more than USD 10,000 million (2016: USD 1,213,785 million; 2015: USD 1,381,567 million).

Conversely, M&A volume failed to sustain two consecutive annual increases as deal making slipped to 26,163 deals in 2017 (2016: 28,577; 2015: 27,132). However, despite the decline, growth was not wholly stripped away as, other than 2016 and 2015, 2017's result was one of the highest recorded since 2006. In all, the volume and value of M&A targeting companies based in Western Europe each accounted for 27 per cent of 2017's 96,082 global deals worth a combined USD 4,740,969 million.

The value of M&A targeting companies based in Asia Pacific rose 3 per cent year-on-year against a 7 per cent decline by volume, to 31,703 deals worth a combined USD 1,415,651 million in 2017, from 34,036 deals totaling USD 1,375,348 million in 2016. Volume declined for the second successive year to a low not recorded since 2014 when there were just 30,792 deals totaling USD 1,223,121 million. However, value in 2017 was the second-highest on record after 2015 (USD 1,864,862 million) and accounted for 30 per cent of the total M&A value recorded globally in 2017 (USD 4,740,969 million).

The volume and value of M&A targeting companies based in the Middle East and North Africa (MENA) decreased in the 12 months of 2017. In all, there were 572 deals worth a combined USD 53,939 million in 2017, representing a decline of 20 per cent in volume and 8 per cent in value year-on-year (2016: 713 deals worth USD 58,911 million). However, despite the disappointing result in terms of value, 2017 was far from a record low, having surpassed 2015 (USD 24,061 million), 2014 (USD 34,246 million) and 2013 (USD 38,796 million), in terms of value.

The volume and value of M&A targeting Central and Eastern Europe (CEE) continued on a downwards trend in 2017, despite companies based in the region being targeted in 16 deals each worth more than USD 1,000 million over the 12 months. In all there were 8,506 deals worth a combined USD 111,668 million recorded for the region, down from 9,385 deals totaling USD 137,382 million in 2016. Russia and CEE deal making accounted for only 8 per cent of 2017's total global volume (96,082) and 2 per cent of value (USD 4,740,969 million) as M&A within the region still lagged behind that of Western Europe, North America and Far East and Central Asia.

Thomson Reuters (2018) points out that despite increased levels of outbound M&A from acquirers based in the United States and intra-Europe M&A activity, cross-border M&A activity totaled US$1.3 trillion during full year 2017, a 10% decline compared to full year 2016 and the slowest year for cross-border M&A since 2014. China Outbound M&A totaled US$141.5 billion, a 35% decline compared to last year's record.

M&A activity for European targets totaled US$867.5 billion during full year 2017, an increase of 17% compared to the level of activity seen during 2016. With US$1.4 trillion in announced deals during 2017, United States M&A fell 16% compared to a year ago, while the United States increased 14% the largest period deals since records began in 1980.

America's M&A volume during full year 2017 was down 8.3% compared to 2016, accruing US$2 trillion in activity from 20,301 announced deals. US Targeted M&A saw a decrease in 2017 from a volume perspective, down 15.6% compared to announced M&A during full year 2016, accruing a total of US$1.4 trillion. Conversely, the number of US targeted transactions announced during full year 2017 reached 13,069 deals, a 13.6% increase from a year ago.

Accumulating US$239.7 billion in transaction value, announced Canadian Involvement activity decreased 6.1% from the totals reached during 2016. Completed Canadian Involvement activity was up 47% compared to full year 2016, driven by the completion of Enbridge Inc's and Spectra Energy Corp's US$43.1 billion merger in Q1.

Announced M&A activity with EMEA involvement totaled US$1.2 trillion from 18,497 deals in 2017, down 2.4% compared to the US$1.3 trillion reached the last year. Announced M&A volume with Asian involvement for full year 2017 decreased by 1.6% to US$1.02 trillion compared to the same period in 2016. 13,516 deals were announced in 2017, a slight increase in deal count from the same period previous year.

Worldwide M&A activity totaled US$4.0 trillion during full year 2018, an increase of 19% compared to full year 2017 and the third annual period to surpass US$4.0 trillion since records began in 1980.

The value of worldwide M&A greater than US$5 billion totaled US$1.5 trillion during full year 2018, an increase of 51% compared to a year ago. One hundred and twenty three deals greater than US$5 billion accounted for 38% of announced M&A activity during the full year 2018, up from 30% during full year 2017. During the second half of 2018, the value of mega deals fell 56% compared to the first half of the year, which ranked as the second largest six-month period for global deal making on record.

Announced M&A activity with EMEA involvement totaled US$1.5 trillion from 17,136 deals in 2018, up 33.9% compared to the US$1.1 trillion reached in the last year. Estimated fees accumulated on EMEA deals completed in 2018 were up 1.8% compared to last year, totaling US$16.5 billion.

Americas M&A volume during 2018 was up 25.6% compared to full year 2017, accruing US$2.4 trillion in activity from 19,249 announced deals. According to estimates, fees generated from completed deals in the Americas totaled US$29.1 billion, a 5.6% increase from fees earned during

2017. US Targeted M&A volume totaled US$1.7 trillion, a 32.1% increase in activity compared to full year 2017. 2018 saw 12,459 deals announced, a 8% decrease from a year ago.

Accumulating US$275.2 billion in transaction value, announced Canadian Involvement activity saw a 15.3% increase from the totals reached during 2017. Completed Canadian Involvement activity was up 8.3% compared to last year. In the Americas, 7 out of the 11 sectors saw an increase in exit multiples during 2018. Overall average EBITDA multiples across industries in the Americas posted a decrease during the period, declining to 14.5x compared to 15x averaged during 2017.

Asian M&A activity in 2018 was the slowest in 3 years, accruing a total of US$950.4 billion, a 4.3% decrease compared to last year's totals. Acquirers headquartered in the US were Asia's most acquisitive companies, with a combined total of US$51.2 billion.

Accumulating US$165 billion in value, announced Australian involvement M&A increased by 39.6% compared to last year's totals, representing the strongest year since 2011. Australian outbound activity reached a six-year high in 2018, accumulating US$26.9 billion from 332 cross-border deals. Deal activity involving Australian companies included 34 deals above US$1 billion, compared to 22 announced in 2017. Australian involvement deals above US$1 billion reached an aggregate total of US$105.7 billion, accounting for 64.1% of the total deal making activity in the region.

With a total value of US$56.1 billion, cross-border China-targeted M&A saw a 23.3% increase compared to 2017 - the highest China inbound M&A activity on record. Conversely, China outbound deal activity accrued US$116.6 billion, a 5.3% decrease from a year ago (Thomson Reuters, 2019).

The value of M&A targeting companies based in Central and Eastern Europe (CEE) increased 29 per cent against a 27 per cent decline by volume in 2018. In total, there were 6,790 deals worth USD 140,265 million announced in the 12 months under review, compared to 9,335 deals worth USD 108,465 million in 2017. In terms of value, 2018 was the highest recorded since 2015, when USD 143,906 million-worth of deals were signed off, and it represents less than 3 per cent of global M&A value for the year (USD 5,303,713 million). The increase by value against the decline in volume suggests buyers favoured individual deals with higher valuations over prolific deal making in 2018, with the increase largely attributable to three CEE deals each worth more than USD 10,000 million in 2018 (Bureau Van Dijk, 2019).

Baker McKenzie, (2018) highlights that 2019 will begin strongly. But rising rates and cooling global growth will follow, so a slowdown in M&A activity is likely in the second half of 2019, followed by a more pronounced easing in 2020, as equity markets pause for breath. There is potential for the start of the next up-cycle thereafter. The predicted total values are USD 2.9 trillion for 2019, falling to USD 2.3 trillion in 2020.

Dealmakers in both the US and Canada have shrugged off concerns over the future of NAFTA and turned in another strong year for both M&A and IPOs in 2018. It is expected another strong year in 2019, as dealmakers respond to the successful conclusion of trilateral trade talks. But with US interest rates potentially on their way back towards a neutral level, and limited scope for further cyclical growth in the economy, the second half of 2019 will see less activity than the first, and 2020 is likely to mark a low in deals.

Several key megadeals are set to complete early in 2019, and US growth looks set to remain around 3% annualized through the first half of the year. But the deal cycle will cool through the latter half of 2019 as the Fed picks up the pace of its exit from quantitative easing (removing liquidity from markets) and GDP growth slows to 2%. Nevertheless, with a strong first half and a cooler second, it is foreseen total M&A to remain at USD 1.4 trillion for 2019 as a whole.

With the Eurozone economy now clearly entering a cyclical slowdown, it can be predicted a relatively substantial easing in M&A activity in 2019, albeit with one cross-border megadeal likely to support the aggregate value. In aggregate, it is foreseen a total M&A in Europe to end 2018 at USD 806 billion, easing to USD 530 billion in 2019, and USD 436 billion the following year.

In Asia Pacific M&A and IPO turned in another strong year in 2018, with dealmakers in the region again focusing on economic fundamentals rather than the potential for disruption to world trade flows. Much of this momentum can be maintained into 2019 despite slower world trade growth, which is key for many economies in the region. More positively, emerging markets look less vulnerable to rising Fed rates than in the past, meaning US monetary policy will drag less on Asia Pacific deal making in 2019 than during previous cycles.

The depreciation of several key currencies in the region (including the RMB) versus the dollar in late 2018 will also undermine the dollar value of Asia-Pacific deals in 2019. It is expected total M&A in the region to rise to USD 751 billion in 2019.

In Latin America domestic M&A was significantly down in 2018, reflecting the political and financial turmoil affecting individual firms' finances as well as the broader economy. However, inbound M&A held up rather better, as did IPO activity, suggesting that particularly overseas investors are taking a longer view. With new governments taking office in Brazil and Mexico, and the resolution of NAFTA uncertainty, it is expected stronger deal making activity in the coming couple of years, with M&A in the region rising to USD 94 billion in 2019 and USD 98 billion in 2020.

With US-Mexico talks successfully concluded – albeit with slightly less favorable terms for Mexico's auto sector – the outlook for business investment and M&A in Mexico is much-improved and it is expected a rebound in M&A in 2019. Argentina's recent agreement with the IMF offers hope for a stabilization in business conditions and economic recovery, though that stabilization is more likely to occur in 2020 than 2019. Meanwhile, in Brazil, the economy is forecast to grow at its fastest rate since 2013 next year, before accelerating further in 2020.

Regarding Middle East and Africa, a recovery in oil prices has helped economies in both regions through 2018, although the global oil market has become more volatile. In the Middle East, continued gradual progress towards more-diversified economies should help build confidence and deal making from 2019 onwards, while in Africa signs of financial and economic stability will do likewise. At USD 38 billion in 2019, total M&A in the two regions will remain impressive in a historical context, albeit with comparisons against 2018 distorted by three megadeals in the UAE.

Chapter 2

MERGERS AND ACQUISITIONS

2.1. WHAT IS THE LOGIC OF M&AS?

Given the rapidly shifting corporate and global landscapes, if we are to keep pace with the speed of change and innovation occurring in the companies that we study, we need to be prepared to maneuver ourselves as researchers engaged in studying one of the most prevalent forms of change in modern corporate history: M&A, as Cartwright, Teerikangas, Rouzies and Wilson-Evered (2012) and DePamphilis (2011) point out. The same point of view is offered by Pignataro (2015) and Trompenaars and Asser (2010) who observe that global business expansion and development through M&As is big business. Furthermore, M&A is a complex and vast topic that takes years of practice to hone and perfect. The study of M&A is highly relevant, as M&A represent a fundamental tool for corporate restructuring (King, Bauer, & Schriber, 2019).

A body of research in international business literature has focused on many reasons to explain the M&As waves. Economic structure, liberalisation and preferential policies, and cultural and legal environment played an important role for attracting FDI as (Picone and Dagnino, 2015; Sahoo, Nataraj, & Dash, 2014) conclude. The authors point out that mergers can increase the combined values of acquirers and projects that could not be financed as stand-alone, while, as these projects are only marginally profitable, diversified firms are less valuable than stand-alone firms.

The almost common view is that M&A is one of the most important business phenomena in the past decades and it will be in the future too. But this does not prevent scholars and practitioners to warn about the M&A dangers (Warter & Warter, 2015b, 2017a). For example, M&A is found to have a statistically significant effect of improving the efficiency of target banks, but not of acquiring banks (Du & Sim, 2016). In their studies, Trompenaars and Asser (2010) and Very, Metais, Lo, and Hourquet (2012) point out that realizing the business benefits and creating wealth in an integration process is not a straightforward procedure. In particular, precise practical predictions of M&A activity can be made at country level and the dependence framework appears appropriate for selecting the possible determinants of M&A activity per country.

In the same direction, Bertrand and Capron (2015) and Reynolds and Teerikangas (2016) remark that international acquisitions actually increase the domestic capabilities of acquiring firms and thus the overall efficiency of home industries as well as the global competitiveness of the investing firm's country. Moreover, instead of the expected difficulty of the cross-border M&A experience, the domestic merger experience ought not be treated as a domestic one, as it is equally affected by the international. For instance, in a competitive global construction industry, construction firms should adopt strategies that give cognizance to the national culture of the countries they intend to work in. However, there was sufficient coverage of single country studies, opposed to cross-cultural and comparative studies (Babatunde & Low, 2015; Gomes, Barnes & Mahmood, 2016).

Acquisition alternatives and their performance are likely influenced by prior investments or cannot be considered independently as Arvanitis, Lokshin, Mohnen, and Woerter (2015) and King (2014) argue. In particular, we find that a larger size of the acquiring firm has a beneficial effect on employment growth, while a larger size of the acquired establishments has an adverse effect (Burghardt & Helm, 2015). Consequently, Almor, Tarba and Margalit (2014) claim that despite their relatively young age, small size, and scarcity of resources and capabilities compared to large technology-based multinational enterprises, born-global companies must use M&As to survive and succeed in a competitive global environment. The findings show that global and host-region firms benefit from cross-border M&A's, whereas home-region firms gain value from product diversification but only up to an inflection point, where further product diversification becomes unmanageable as (Kling, Ghobadian, Hitt, Weitzel, & O'Regan, 2014) point out.

Another interesting opinion on organizational change and employee mobility is offered by Seo and Hill (2005) and Younge, Tong and Fleming (2015). They argue that M&A necessarily involves organizational change, integrating some or all parts of the original organizations' functions and activities. In addition, employee mobility is an important factor affecting acquirers' decision to use M&A's as a strategy to source knowledge and human capital from target firms.

To sum up, M&A is a multilevel, multidisciplinary, and multistage process which requires a pluralist approach, as Galpin (2018) and Warter and Warter (2014a) argue. M&A researchers have focused generically separately on pre-acquisition factors and post-acquisition influential factors. Neither scholars nor practitioners have a comprehensive understanding of the factors involved in the M&A process and their interrelationships. It can therefore be concluded that M&A's are clearly the most important forms of change in the modern economic world, a complex area who requires an interdisciplinary approach. Although M&A has received increasing scholarly attention in the last decades, this topic remains a scholarly puzzle and a practical challenge.

2.2. M&A PERFORMANCE - SUCCESS OR FAILURE?

Despite all efforts there is no commonly acknowledged 'correct' concept of M&A performance yet. There is also a considerable debate about the validity of the data from which this concept was derived. Historically, M&A researchers have focused separately on pre-acquisition factors and post-acquisition factors influencing performance. Meanwhile, it is less clear whether poor performance and value destruction is due to the acquisition or to other factors (DePamphilis, 2011; Gomes, Angwin, Weber, & Tarba, 2013, Warter & Warter, 2018a). M&A performance is primarily affected by specific M&A characteristics, but not by general market characteristics such as demand development or competition conditions as Arvanitis and Stucki (2014) and Meglio (2009) remark. For example, although the realm of technology-driven M&As play a prominent role in changing the landscape of several industries, M&A performance in low-tech and service industries deserves further attention. Astonishingly, M&A performance is not affected by firm size.

Moreover, firm size, firm age, wages, turnover and the export intensity are accounted for in the pre-acquisition period, since all can be assumed to affect the probability of experiencing a takeover and performance measures in the post-acquisition period (Geluebcke, 2015). In addition, during the crisis, certain characteristics of the firms like the relative size of the target, cross-border nature of deals, acquirer's cash reserves and friendly nature of deals are important determinants of long-term post-M&A operating performance as Rao-Nicholson, Salaber and Cao (2016) and Travers (2004) conclude. Accordingly, when a proposed merger falls apart, though, it is likely that the price of the stock of the company being acquired will fall.

Some practitioners and scholars have postulated that the shortage of communication channels or the amateurish use of communications can become a barrier in negotiation, decision-making, and planning. However, the understanding of networks practiced by acquired ventures can increase buyers' accessibility and visibility to target opportunities and improve M&A outcomes (Dashti & Schwartz, 2015; Warter & Warter, 2015a).

The common underlying belief is that M&A performance has a strong influence on M&A's decisions. I strongly believe that the most important problem is the misunderstanding of the M&A performance concept itself. Some authors (Chatterjee, 2009; Drees, 2014) consider that where alliances have more short-term effects, M&A's create more value in the long-run, which implies that when firms first consider an acquisition programme, a common theme is a clear strategic analysis of the market they are considering. Other authors (Bauer & Matzler, 2014; Marks & Mirvis, 2011) highlight that the Merger Syndrome is a fusion of uncertainty and the likelihood of change which hampers integration, reduces productivity, and contributes to turnover of key people. Consequently, M&A success is a function of strategic complementarity, cultural fit, and the degree of integration.

The complexity of the M&As process has generated several challenges to making M&As a success and meeting target expectations. Strictly controlled and inter-linked components relating to the business evaluation process have a significant impact on the outcome of the cross- border transactions (Bodner & Capron, 2018; Hassan, Chidlow & Romero-Martinez, 2016; Warter & Warter, 2015d, 2017b). In comprehensive articles (Gomes et al., 2013; Meglio, 2009) generally agree with previous authors and notice that the high failure rate of mergers and acquisitions suggests that neither scholars nor practitioners have a thorough understanding of the variables involved in the M&A process and their complex interrelationships. Since post-merger performance is difficult to measure, the authors' conclusion is that findings provide evidence that a serious reflection on construct measurement is needed.

The existing literature is characterized by several independent streams of management research that either have studied discrete variables in the preacquisition or post acquisition phase. The conclusion is that in this way, an interdisciplinary approach to M&A is outlined. Recent work (Bebenroth, 2015) remarks that organizational identification depends on the type of employees, whether regular or not will influence the organizational identification which will influence the performance of the M&A. To summarize, M&A success depends on mechanisms that enhance the exploration and exploitation of knowledge as Reus (2012) concludes. Hence, when choosing a company to acquire, whose knowledge is desired, the acquirer's management must examine the similarities in knowledge and culture (Calipha, Brock, Rosenfeld, & Dvir, 2018).

A merger is a dramatic event for companies and employees, for it requires integration of two organizations. Mergers and acquisitions (M&As) have inevitably drawn the attention of many groups of scholars, each of whom studies the subject from a unique perspective. For example, Dezi,

Battisti, Ferraris and Papa (2018) consider that more research is necessary to examine M&A operations under the wider approach of open innovation. Others (Teerikangas, & Reynolds, 2018) consider that the value of ethnography in the merger context lies in what the things we learn about the organization, its culture and its employees tell us about how they handle the process of joining with another firm. Most surveys on M&A point to a success rate of about one third. The M&A reasons, as they emerge from this review, can be described as a result of globalisation, of the need of growth and of achieving synergies. The M&A process can be described as multilevel, multidisciplinary, and multistage phenomenon. M&A researchers have focused generically separately on pre-acquisition factors and post-acquisition influential factors. Neither scholars nor practitioners have a comprehensive understanding of the factors involved in the M&A process and their influence on merger performance.

2.3. The Most Important Intercultural Issues in M&As

Since the end of the Cold War, the study of intercultural relations has become a popular topic in the field of global politics and economics. For example, between 2002 and 2004, Lodorfos and Boateng conducted 32 interviews with senior managers of 16 European large scale M&A deals in the chemical industry and also found out that culture "plays a key role in the integration process and consequently the overall success of the M&A." I agree with one of the course conclusion that is neither should one make the mistake to blame intercultural problems for every M&A failure and nor should the topic be over- or underestimated. It is important to find the right balance between strategic, financial and cultural aspects (Rongxing, 2012; Rothlauf, 2011).

Regarding intercultural relations, Rkibi (2009) argues that the scholars seem to be concerned rather with strategy and structure to the detriment of intercultural relations, while intercultural approach proposes, ultimately, achieving a reasonable compromise between partners compromise on the basis of which lies the knowledge, understanding and integrating differences in realistic and reasonable strategies by which can be correctly solved problems of this class. People in various fields work beyond borders. Therefore, one should not overlook the need to learn Intercultural Communication. Business partners might be better off dealing with entrepreneurs who are influenced by different cultures, if they are aware of these cultural influences and their implications for business practice and entrepreneurial behaviours (Liu and Almor, 2016; Raddawi, 2015).

An objectivist understanding of culture considers it as a relatively stable system of norms, values, and behaviour patterns. Empirical research confirmed that each of a large number of single items that are viewed as values across cultures could be subsumed under the heading of one of the following 10 basic values: universalism, benevolence, tradition, conformity, security, power, achievement, hedonism, stimulation, and self-direction (Doring et al., 2014; Vauclair et al., 2015). One should take into account personal values, when the goal is to understand and predict moral attitudes and judgments across cultures.

According to Gesteland (2012), whether marketing, selling, sourcing, negotiating or managing internationally, the differences between relationship-focused (RF) and deal-focused (DF) business behavior impact our success throughout the global marketplace. The most disappointing comparison of cross-cultural measures that are supposed to be identical, but are not, is that of the national indices for Big-Five personality traits as Minkov, Bond and Blagoev (2015) argue.

In two interesting papers (Barmeyer & Mayrhofer, 2008; Bird & Mendenhall, 2016) is highlighted that intercultural management attempts to evaluate the influence of culture (national and organisational) on the perceptions, interpretations and actions of managers in cross-border M&As. Often, underestimation of the cultural factor seems surprising, because the merging of companies is, above all, a merging between different human beings. In the same vein, Durand (2016) remarks that managerial perceptions may be affected in different ways, depending on the middle manager's background (experience, age, religion, status, experience of M&A's, and past experiences with other cultures).

Culture can influence in a decisive manner the individual's attitude to research in his various stages of development, education and training. Noticeably, not all culture is defined in terms of its members' psychological features, nor perhaps should it be. Crossvergence practices can be conducive to further affect the adaptation process by recognizing the common ground that exists for cultural training and mutual learning from a cross-cultural perspective (Bond, 2014; Xing, Liu, Tarba, & Cooper, 2016).

Other scholars (Dundon, 2002; Rosinski, 2003) support the previous ideas showing that within groups there are individual differences, class and educational differences, ethnic and racial differences, personality type differences, and gender differences. Thereby, it is important to understand the difference between the stated culture and the real culture that relies more on the personalities and behaviors of the individuals than on a list of desired attributes. The organization's culture—its values, norms, and preferred styles—as well as its structures and systems, provide the container in which individuals interact and interpret their experience. Gender may also influence how individuals react to supportive features of the working environment in shaping their work investment decisions (Ferdman, n.d.; Lu, Huang and Bond, 2016).

Moreover, language is the medium used by M&A integration team members to have conversation with others. Therefore, a common linguistic background (e.g., English, French, German, etc.) is vital for communication and knowledge transfer, as M&A process is a very difficult and complex activity. Thus, because virtual team members are located in different countries and speech communities, they must rely on a common language and communication technology to solve organizational tasks (Klitmøller, Schneider & Jonsen, 2015). Other scholars (Gomes et al., 2014; Xing et al., 2014) point out that based on their analysis, cultural influences at the macro level can affect HRM practices at the organizational level. Cultural forces affect the kind of leader behaviour that is usually accepted, enacted, and effective within a collective. The perceptions of the cultural differences and the political interferences in the M&A activities in the host economies need to be effectively managed by the acquirers as (Arvey, Dhanaraj, Javidan, & Zhang, 2015; Rao-Nicholson, Khan and Stokes, 2016) argue.

One of the major shortcomings in the research of intercultural particularities in M&A is revealed by Teerikangas, Very and Pisano (2011) and Viegas-Pires (2013). They conclude that cultural change in cross-border acquisitions not only occurs at the level of organizational culture, but also at the level of national culture. In sum, there is a need to consider interactions between multiple culture levels and extra cultural factors (i.e., the different dimensions of integration). In Trompenaars and Asser (2010) by now classic study, is concluded that organizations will have problems if they fail to identify and focus on the key issues or to question (cultural) assumptions or fail to assess and allocate appropriate resources. Moreover, most scholars and practitioners intuitively feel that cultural differences matter in M&A, but when they matter, under what conditions they matter, and how they matter are at the moment poorly understood. Consequently, mergers and acquisitions across national borders have become frequent, but they remain a regular source of cross-cultural clashes (Hofstede, Hofstede & Minkov, 2010; Ulijn, Duysters & Meijer, 2010).

Cultural particularities happen to be especially relevant in M&A because different cultures must be integrated into a single one, or one culture has to be absorbed by the other. Cultural integration takes lots of time, energy, and money unforeseen by the financial practitioners who designed the merger. As a matter of fact, in a M&A process, a significant aspect is bringing together distinct management groups from different cultures, attached to different management styles. For instance, study of new forms of communication in M&As could benefit from ethnographic observation of "unintended" communication through video recordings of virtual meetings to examine nonverbal communication that is at variance with verbal or that has different meanings across cultures (Sarala, Vaara., & Junni, 2017).

A similar point of view is presented by Arvey et al. (2015) and Gertsen, Soederberg and Vaara (2004). They show that not only researchers but also the managers and employees involved in mergers have pointed to national and organizational cultural differences as major causes of integration problems. One can predict that the cultural differences will be there for a long time, and managers from different cultures are required to adapt to each other when they do cross-border M&A.

This review revealed various interpretations of intercultural particularities. Consequently, it can be noticed that most scholars and practitioners agreed that cultural influences matter in M&A. It can be concluded that any management and research approach should consider the significant role of national and organizational cultural differences, neglecting the cultural factor can be a huge mistake.

Regarding the relationships between cultural differences, cultural integration, and M&A performance, Rothlauf (2011) and Trompenaars and Asser (2010) reveal that in most studies the main reason given for merger failure is "cultural differences." The authors also state, that crucial for the success of the cultural integration is not a high number of similarities, since even M&A between apparently similar partners but the identification of conflict potential and their consideration during the integration process.

An interesting approach is presented by Ahammad et al. (2014) and Rkibi (2009). The authors argue that greater national cultural distance and organizational culture differences enhances the competitive advantage of the combined firm and eventually, post-acquisition performance. On the other hand, studies have shown that a multicultural group shows more creativity and has a greater ability to find various solutions to problems. In general, the shock in the case of cultures of comparisons is exerted at three main levels: structure and operating systems, management style and mode of legitimation of power within entities. Accordingly, international business education should include seminars that focus on awareness of differences in cross-cultural business communication as well as on culture-specific discourse systems that have an impact on business communication (Meier & Schier, 2009; Zaidman, 2001).

In the literature on performance in M&A, different effects of cultural differences have been identified. For instance, Bingham, Heimeriks, Schijven, and Gates (2014) found consistent statistical patterns suggesting positive performance effects of experience in the context of acquisitions. Other researchers (Manos, Drori, Shoham, & Aharonson, 2015) highlight that societal aspirations, the difference between cultural value score and the related practice score of uncertainty avoidance and future orientation have a positive effect on the national savings rate. Still others (Zait, Warter and Warter, 2014) emphasize that mixing different solutions as cultural origin offers almost always the chance of obtaining a significant intercultural synergy in business, management etc. In sum, in M&As meeting among professionals is, first of all, meeting in specific conditions, among more or less different cultures.

He (2009) and Stahl and Voigt (2005) too reflect upon this phenomenon and claim that cultural differences, if properly understood and managed, can be an asset rather than a liability in M&A, and that cultural differences may affect the sub-processes of task integration and socio-cultural integration in different ways. To phrase it differently, the acquisition process may affect performance, as acquiring companies adopting a 'soft approach' or introducing 'gradual changes' are more probable to gain knowledge of the subsidiary progressively. Performance of M&A's depends upon the quality of socio-cultural integration processes. Trompenaars and Asser (2010), in their conceptual paper, consider that organizations that are able to reconcile their differences will have created competitive advantage. If they do not, they will end up amongst the 70% of mergers that fail.

This study seeks to further the understanding of the impact of cultural differences on M&A performance with emphasis on cross border M&A. Therefore, it searched in the scientific literature different opinions to clarify these matters, as described above. Despite the fact that a growing field of analysis has been directed at the implications of cultural differences for the M&A performance the results have remained debatable.

It is not surprising for experienced scholars and practitioners that cultural differences also play an important role in the M&A process and, also, are of critical importance to successful integration of merging firms. In papers on the relationship between cultural differences and M&A performance, Reus (2012) and Stahl and Voigt (2005) remark that cross-border M&As have double-layered cultural differences of organizational and national differences. While some studies found that cultural differences were negatively associated with post-acquisition performance regardless of the integration approach taken and contrary to expectations, several studies revealed a positive relationship between cultural differences and M&A performance.

The difficulties and controversies of these processes are analysed, also, by other authors. Hofstede et al. (2010) and Trompenaars and Asser (2010) point out that cross-border acquisitions are a fast way of expanding, but their cultural risk is considerable. Being able to dissect human activity and communication is a serious attempt to identify and measure the value of human relationships and trust in M&As. I agree with the authors when they conclude that it is advisable for potential cross-border acquisitions to be preceded by an analysis of the cultures of the corporation and of the acquisition candidate. Most studies show that more than half of M&As do not prove to be successful. Traditionally, scholars and practitioners focused on 'hard' features like financial and strategic features for explaining the success or failure of M&As. More recently, however, research into more 'soft' features such as organizational and human resources have increased in importance due to the fact that the aspects of human nature and of social functioning that shape individual value priorities are widely shared across cultures (Schwartz, 2012; Ulijn et al., 2010).

The positive influence of organizational cultural differences described in previous studies can be explained by increased resource flexibility in employee skills: organizational cultural differences provide a broader skill base for the employees in the combined firm as Sarala, Junni, Cooper, and Tarba (2014) remark or by a cultural legitimacy, gained and maintained by M&A involved organizations, in their surrounding organizational environment as Rottig (2013) points out. Cultural differences can, however, impede structural integration if structural integration is done in a manner that is in conflict with the existing culture of the acquired firm. The successful approach adds careful attention to how a combination advances the business strategy of a firm, due diligence on behavioral and cultural factors that might complicate the combination, and a clear picture of how the firms will be integrated (Golesorkhi, Mersland, Randøy, & Shenkar, 2019; Marks & Mirvis, 2011; Teerikangas & Laamanen, 2014). The results obtained by G. Hofstede whatever country that is part of, any individual has a different view regarding the definition of correct behavior, reasonable and adequate (Veiss

& Abrudan, 2012). Therefore, Warter and Warter (2014b, 2018b) consider that cultural diversity in organizations can be both an asset and a liability. Whether the losses associated with cultural diversity can be minimized and the gains be realized will depend likewise on the managers' ability to manage the M&A processes in an effective manner.

Because the culture clusters are important for this analysis, a few words on the background.

The culture clusters are developed by Huib Wursten. It is the result of the experience in coping with issues of global companies. It is the combination of the first four confirmed dimensions of Geert Hofstede. Wursten realized that for methodological purposes it is important to show that the dimensions found in empirical research are independent. For application of the findings in real life it is however a necessity to show that the 4 dimensions have an influence on each other and one cannot explain reality by looking at the dimensions one by one. The combinations make a different "Gestalt" meaning that the whole is more than the sum of separate elements. Wursten defined 6 different combinations. These are called the 6 culture clusters covering for 99% of the differences between countries in the world. The 6 culture clusters are different in the sense that they can be described as having special outlooks on society and even different ways of thinking. The different outlook and ways of thinking lead to different "rules of the game." Wursten calls this as "Mental Images." Japan is not fitting one of the culture clusters. They have their own Mental Image. So in summary: 6 culture clusters are found and 7 Mental Images (Wursten, 2017).

Although many scholars and practitioners consider that cultural differences play an important role in M&AS, they are often underestimated or the conditions are poorly understood. Some scholars consider that cultural differences may affect the M&A process while others remark a positive effect in M&A performance based on synergy creation. The relationship between intercultural elements and M&A performance is a key topic in literature in last two decades.

The picture emerging from the findings shows a lack of consensus about the intercultural particularities in M&A. On the same time, the common underlying belief of many scholars and practitioners is that intercultural aspects have a strong influence on M&A performance. Despite the advances, important research gaps and paradoxes remain. In sum, these contradictory findings suggest that the intercultural issues require more theoretical and empirical study and that cultural differences in organizations can be both an asset and a liability.

Chapter 3

The Significance of Post-Investment Phase

3.1. Why Is the Post-Investment Phase So Critical for M&As?

The integration process in the post-merger stage is a crucial phase where value is created or not. Therefore, many companies, managers and others professionals invest an enormous amount of time and energy in fostering depth and speed of integration (see, for instance, Bauer, Schriber, Degischer, & King, 2018), build on their previous integration experiences and meticulously plan future integration processes. Moreover, while overpayment and poor strategy are among the most common explanations for the failure of M&As, numerous studies support the conclusion that rapid integration efforts are more likely to result in mergers that achieve the acquirer's expectations (Bauer, Hautz & Matzler, 2015; DePamphilis, 2012).

According to De Bernardis and Giustiniano (2015) and Peltokorpi, Allen and Froese (2015) in the post-merger phases, the strategic autonomy of the pre-existing companies could respond to a specific organizational and business strategy, and therefore be accepted by the top management. Nevertheless, two individuals with comparable perceived sacrifices associated with leaving may perceive the risks of making those sacrifices differently and thus be more or less likely to develop turnover intentions. In addition, top managers and key persons are often restricted in the range of behavioural outcomes caused by emotions (Hassett, Reynolds, & Sandberg, 2018). Moreover, in the context of M&A decisions, recent findings of Firk, Maybuechen, Oehmichen, & Wolff (2018) indicate the positive effect of value-based management on M&A returns is contingent upon the risk that managers pursue self-interested decisions.

An interesting point of view (Ahammad, Glaister, Weber, & Tarba, 2012; Ahammad, Tarba, Liu, & Glaister, 2016) mentions that the departure of an acquired firm's top managers is considered to be an important determinant of poor post-acquisition performance. The conclusion of the authors is that few scholars and managers appear to understand either the underlying causes of this turnover or how it should be managed.

Angwin and Meadows (2014) and Rottig (2013) emphasise also a similar opinion: their cluster analysis supports a recasting of the dominant post-acquisition integration strategy typology to more fully recognize the flavour of frameworks from other perspectives-which includes post-acquisition top management retention or dismissal- and to reflect the new integration strategies. In other words, in this period, the combined workforces must work together effectively, and the expected goals and objectives of the transaction (such as, for example, creation of synergies, etc.) are to be achieved. Łupina-Wegener, Schneider and van Dick (2015) introduce the concept of optimal shared identity, defined as the employees' shared belonging to the post-merger organization in the face of salient outgroups. Cultural effects occur when people interact, and most interactions of employees occur in the post-merger integration phase. Hence, different roles of similarity and status at successive stages of post-merger integration would imply that these factors should be seen as complementary explanation of individuals' reactions and behaviour in cross-border M&As (Bauer, Matzler & Wolf, 2016; Yildiz, 2016).

Many authors analyse the post-investment stage and its implications (Brogiato, 2012; Geluebcke, 2015; Kim, Haleblian & Finkelstein, 2011; Weber & Drori, 2011). The integration phase is always critical as two entities that were used to be separated now have to behave accordingly to the same guidelines, missions and mentalities but many of the problems associated with the post-merger integration of two firms can be avoided or managed if identification with the merger is analysed and coordinated. Meanwhile, some results point to an average employment decrease and no productivity improvements following a cross-border M&A and the fact that the experience of managers may allow a firm to overcome an inclination to overpay for acquisitions. Other scholars (Seo & Hill, 2005; Straub, 2007) show that M&As are relative complex events that involve the interaction of a large number of company life variables and are insufficiently comprehend. On the other hand, some sources of problems, such as blending of different organizational identities and cultures, are relatively unique to M&As.

An interesting point of view is expressed by Weber and Tarba (2013). They show that a novel post-acquisition integration approach, namely light-touch integration, is investigated, and supported by newly assembled empirical evidence in the context of Chinese M&As in Germany. Light-touch integration essentially synthesizes the preservation and symbiosis integration approaches due to the contextual characteristics of Chinese cross-border M&As and facilitates the activities involved in implementing of the post-acquisition phase. As Gomes et al. (2013) observe, cultural differences have been identified at multiple levels of analysis including National, Regional, Industrial, Company, and Professional levels. However, the interrelationships among corporate culture, national culture, and integration approaches, as well as their influence on the success of international acquisitions, are not clear and can even be contradictory. In order to cope with these complex relationships, Weber, Tarba and Reichel (2009, 2011) suggest a model where integration approaches should consider corporate and national culture differences and synergy potential.

The assumption behind post-M&As typologies is that the higher the need for integration, the higher the degree of change required in organizational culture and identity, management systems and HR practices. Consequently, the leadership and talent retention are critical people-related themes in post-M&A integration, but the extent to which these factors interact with each other and contribute to the success of post-M&A

integration is under-researched (Gomes, Angwin, Peter, & Mellahi, 2012; Zhang et al., 2014).

The integration phase is critical due to the significant cultural differences of the two different organisations. Their influence is not clear and sometimes contradictory. Many scholars have argued that is difficult to analyse post-merger integration.

3.2. Integration Issues

An emerging and growing field of research has investigated the integration issues in M&A due to the fact the integration process is critical in cross-border M&A. It is difficult to analyze post-merger integration, because there are different manners of interpreting and reconstructing the integration process. If culture is often considered as an obstacle to the success of M&As, other authors argue that cultural distance can enhance the performance of cross-border acquisitions by providing access to the partner's routines and repertoires embedded in national culture. Four main unresolved issues were identified: linking pre- and post-merger processes, the role of culture, the role of prior acquisition experience, and how to assess performance (Barmeyer & Mayrhofer, 2008; Stahl et al., 2013).

The findings are not clear, part of the explanation for unresolved issues is that most studies have considered the different dimensions of integration equally. Galpin and Herndon (2014) and Weber et al., (2009) argue that in addition to integration process and operational measures, measures of the effectiveness of cultural integration should also be developed and implemented. In sum, cultural differences, whether organizational or national, show different relationship to level of integration. The directions of these relationships are contradictory, and the influence on performance is indefinite. Historically, many hold the view that to integrate fully, a newly acquired business takes a period of between five and seven years (CCPS, 2010).

Acquisitions present a special challenge for the management attempting to develop specific capabilities for managing the pre- and post-merger stages

(Weber, Rachman-Moore & Tarba, 2012; Colman & Grøgaard, 2013). In line with the authors, it can be argued that because mergers and acquisitions occur relatively infrequently and unpredictably, the ability of management to accumulate considerable amounts of observations needed to capitalize on simple mechanisms is limited. In a post-merger integration process, expanding and transforming group boundaries may challenge or threaten identity on an organizational level, and individuals' feelings of belonging and identification with the organization on the individual level. This concern is also discussed by Yildiz (2014), who points out that incorporating theories of social psychology on status characteristics can also be useful to challenge the widely-held belief that sociocultural integration is a desired end-result in M&As, which by and large reflects itself with the eradication of so-called "us versus them" thinking.

Gouveia, Vione, Milfont, and Fischer (2015) found evidence showing that basic values change over the life course broadly in line with psychosocial development. As part of the adoption of English as a lingua franca language fluency had quite significant, and in some senses dramatic, effects on post-merger integration (Kroon, Cornelissen & Vaara, 2016). Other authors' findings (Hanges, Aiken, Park, & Su, 2016; Zhang et al., 2015) suggest that strategic decisions are made by the leaders. Because post-merger M&A integration is a strategic decision, employees are not granted autonomy in strategic decision-making, and thus the empowering leadership style is not appropriate during post- merger integration.

A greater difference in management style may lead to more significant cultural clashes and to difficulties in the integration. It is therefore important for foreign acquiring companies to be more cautious in introducing changes in these two management areas (He, 2009).

In their studies on integration in M&As, He (2009) and Whitaker (2012) observe that every integration is unique, but studies have confirmed a few key reasons mergers underperform or fail outright: conflicting goals and strategies, poor communication, conflict, and disparate cultures. A greater difference in management style may lead to more significant cultural clashes and to difficulties in the integration. Harikkala-Laihinen, Hassett, Raitis, and Nummela (2018) remark that interactive forms of communication are most beneficial for socio-cultural integration. For instance, what is more unique to the African context is that regional differences are accentuated, and may often have a deeper impact on the integration challenges following domestic and international deals (Ellis, Lamont, Reus, & Faifman, 2015).

It is likely that when a lower level of integration is initially sought, this would reduce spillover concerns, meaning that any subsequent oscillation would be less amplified and thus recoupling after compartmentalization would be more possible. In addition, an organization cannot succeed with multiple irreconcilable ways of working (Marks et al., 2014; Sinha, Daellenbach & Bednarek, 2015). It has been suggested by DePamphilis (2012) and Hajro (2014) that the post-merger integration organization should consist of a management integration team and a series of integration work teams that take into account that the formation of interpersonal relationships, trust and shared identity in turn has an influence on the levels of cooperation, resistance, perceived stress and the turnover rate.

In contrast with the previous authors, an interesting opinion belonging to Vaara, Junni, Sarala, Ehrnrooth, and Koveshnikov (2013) reveals that special attention should be focused on how managers may overemphasize the role of cultural differences and even deliberately blame cultural differences for failure. At the same time, other causes of integration problems might pass unnoticed and be left unaddressed. Cross-border M&As more often may have a "triple-layered" acculturation challenge where national, regional, and organizational cultural differences play a role, which places extraordinary cultural strain on management in integration processes. In addition, the numerous coexisting subcultures play a role in the complex processes of post-merger integration (Ellis et al., 2015; Van Marrewijk, 2016). For example, the difficulties in the M&A stages, especially integration phase, may be more easily overcome with a strong historical anchor embedded in the corporate culture (Warter & Warter, 2015e).

In a processual approach, Hitt and Pisano (2003) and Weber, Tarba and Rozen Bachar (2012) examines the need to better understand the effects of cultural and institutional differences on the post-merger integration process and on the success of cross-border M&As. Furthermore, each M&A requires a 'tailor-made' post-merger integration approach and an appropriate implementation due to the fact that an inappropriate post-merger integration approach or an inadequate degree of implementation can negatively affect M&A performance (Teerikangas & Thanos, 2017).

Despite this substantial body of research on mergers, there is little evidence on how integration is accomplished. Some practitioners consider that organizational integration is difficult and costly, and mergers are implemented in ways that mitigate those costs.

3.3. What Is the Connection between Integration and M&A Success?

Authors exploring the connection between integration and M&A performance in M&As tend to rely on diverse theories. An interesting view (Gomes et al., 2013; Stahl & Voigt, 2005) expresses that in essence, cultural differences seem to matter but it is not clear whether these can be handled in a beneficial way. Very important is to capture the degree of conflict and strain at the sociocultural level, a critical indicator of M&A success or failure from the perspective of the employees and the organization as a whole. For instance, according to Proft (2014) the pace of integration depends on the type of integration. The author replaced the question "Is speed of integration beneficial to M&A success" with "Which type of speed of integration is beneficial for M&A success?"

How do we measure M&A performance? This is a leading question in much M&A research from the 1990's to the present (e.g., Kang, Woo, Burton, & Mitchell 2018). Some scholars, such as Chatterjee and Brueller (2015) and Meglio and Risberg (2011) state that the main problem with M&A performance research would be the lack of clarity in constructing the different measures and a widespread tendency to compare incomparable results in a quest to find variables explaining the variance in performance. Other scholars, such as Marks et al., (2014) and U. Zander and L. Zander (2010) consider that it is imperative to face the complexity of integrating international acquisitions today while retaining sight of crucial questions such as what type of cultural differences specifically influences the integration process. When effectively managed, cultural distinctions can enrich the integration process and lead to a durable combination of the two firms. For instance, an interesting study (CCPS, 2010) points out that language and local culture are two of the most significant barriers to successful integration that need to be overcome in any M&A activity.

Based on the empirical findings, specific national and organizational cultural categories have a significant impact on specific socio-cultural integration processes such as the creation of interpersonal relationships, trust and shared identity. The formation of interpersonal relationships, trust and shared identity in turn has an influence on the levels of cooperation, resistance, perceived stress and the turnover rate (Hajro, 2015; Stiles et al., 2015; Zhang et al., 2015). In sum, Chatterjee and Brueller (2015) conclude that typically, challenges to post-merger performance arise from several primary factors: the breadth or pervasiveness of the resource interactions across the value chain of the acquiring and acquired firms, a cultural mismatch or the scale of the acquisition.

Some scholars consider cultural differences an obstacle to the merger integration. By contrast, other scholars pointed to the fact that cultural distance can enhance the M&A performance in the post-merger phase. Even though accounting measures seem to be the preferred choice for many scholars, not everybody considers them to be optimal to measure performance. Other scholars prefer to capture the degree of conflict at the organisation level.

Some scholars and practitioners argue, for instance, that the key integration challenges are alignment of cultures and motivation of employees. This review also reveals that other scholars and practitioners overemphasize the role of cultural differences and even blame for every failure. Collectively, these findings suggest that further research on post-merger integration is required.

Chapter 4

INTERCULTURAL SYNERGY

4.1. WHAT ARE THE FACETS OF INTERCULTURAL SYNERGY?

Some studies, such as Calipha, Tarba and Brock (2012) and Li Destri, Picone and Mina (2012) define synergy, in business usage, as the ability of two or more units or companies to generate greater value working together than they could working apart. Generally, the justification of M&A operations is the intention to create positive synergies. Nevertheless, in only 8% of the observations the estimates of the synergy include forecasts of revenue enhancements as a result of the merger. In particular, firms are better able to achieve synergy when the institutions of the host country are more similar to the institutions in the acquiring firm's home country (Dutordoir, Roosenboom & Vasconcelos, 2014; Hitt et al., 2009).

These results raise questions about the efforts invested in exploiting the synergy potential. High degree of integration may be needed to exploit high levels of synergy, but a high degree of integration may cause intense culture clash and human resource problems that can ruin the merger performance. An interesting point of view of the way of reaching success in M&As belongs to Larsson and Finkelstein (1999) and Trompenaars and Asser (2010). The authors consider that the success of a merger or acquisition is gauged by the degree of synergy realization rather than potentially ambiguous criteria such as accounting, market returns etc. For instance, stock swap mergers may signal that bidder insiders are offering their company stock as acquisition currency when they are overvalued or when the merger synergies are uncertain or difficult to estimate and extract (Ismail, 2011).

Evaluating the synergies and savings for any merger or acquisition will confirm the direction the involved parties need to take and determine the steps and processes to be used. It is also extremely important if we can identify the dominant process by which takeover gains are realized-synergy or restructuring- it may be possible to argue the merits or demerits of rejecting a takeover offer (Chatterjee, 1992; Trompenaars & Asser, 2010). Other scholar (Harris, 2004) claim that cultural synergy builds upon similarities and fuses differences resulting in more effective human activities and systems. Post-acquisition synergies appear to be essentially rooted in the social relations and interactions that emerge between organizational members. Synergy expectations are positively related to announcement period returns, longer-term performance, and the market's reaction to quarterly earnings announcements (Cicon, Clarke, Ferris, & Jayaraman, 2014; Mirc, 2012).

In a comprehensive analysis of the synergy measurement model, Clougherty and Duso (2011) and Garzella and Fiorentino (2014) consider that timing is an influential factor in synergy assessment, but synergies take longer to achieve than expected. Likewise, the authors point to the proclivity of scholarship to neglect the potential role of collusive synergies. Research suggests that identifying the gains from mergers is a difficult task and up to 65% of failed mergers and acquisitions are due to 'people issues,' i.e., intercultural differences causing communication breakdowns that result in poor productivity. This disappointment occurs because a deeper analysis of the systematic culture of the organization is overlooked (Arikawa & Takechi, 2012; Desai, Joshi & Joshi, n.d.; Warter & Warter, 2015g).

Differences in national culture can create a source of conflict and misunderstanding that prevents the involved companies from successful cooperation. This is in line with Hofstede's hypothesis of cultural distance in which he argues that the difficulties and risks associated with cross-cultural contact increase with growing cultural differences between organizations. However, the opposite view, that differences in national culture between the partnering organizations can be beneficial, leading to potential synergy, has also been advanced and empirically supported by many scholars and practitioners (Chatterjee, 2007; Ulijn et al., 2010).

Through this analysis, it was revealed that many different factors may shape the intercultural synergy. Despite a growing body of research on synergy creation, it can be concluded that the concept of "intercultural synergy" is still poorly understood. The question whether there is a need to deepen the research on intercultural synergy can only receive a positive response.

4.2. What Is the Impact of Intercultural Synergy on Human Integration in M&A?

The extent to which a merger or acquisition resulted in synergistic gains was related to the strategic potential of the merger, the degree of organizational integration after the deal was completed, and the lack of employee resistance to the integration of the joining companies, as Larsson and Finkelstein (1999) and Marks and Mirvis (2010) argue. A different view (Harrison, Hitt & Ireland, 1991; Zaheer, Castañer & Souder, 2013) reveals that certain conditions (e.g., when complementarity rather than similarity is the primary source of synergy) lead to high levels of both integration and autonomy. In fact, only cultural differences were found to have positive effects on post-acquisition performance.

It is critical to understand the importance of intercultural synergy when working or managing within multinational organizations in order to be able to take advantage of the potential synergies. Within such a context, global leaders who promote intercultural synergy influence social change in human behaviour and improve system effectiveness (Harris, 2004; Nair, Demirbag & Mellahi, 2015). For instance, Trompenaars and Asser (2010) consider that people succeed in achieving synergies, not because they are good at choosing one side over the other, but because they are able to reconcile seemingly opposing values.

In a reflection on synergy creation in the integration process, Cho and La (2014) and Meglio, King and Risberg (2015) point out that the horizontal integration type, occurring between two similar businesses, has the strongest potential to achieve synergy creation. Even if the goals of human integration may be clearly set by top managers, the timing and methods for achieving them may become a source of continuous tension for the employees involved in the integration process. In approaching the topic of M&A performance, the key to understanding the dynamics underlying the performance of M&A is the comparison between the amount of premium of acquisition and the value of synergies that a business combination generates. Promoting synergy in and through the organization is one of the characteristics of the new work or knowledge culture (Harris, 2004; Li Destri et al., 2012).

In a paper on the relationship between synergy potential and cultural differences Weber, Tarba and RozenBachar (2011) reveal that the fit of integration approach mediates the relationship between synergy potential and cultural differences and makes possible the achievement of synergy benefits during the integration process. But, how do we measure cultural differences?. Rosinski (2003) proposes an integrative framework, the "Cultural Orientations Framework" (COF), which maps out regions of cultural territory and has a number of uses: assess cultural differences, bridge different cultures etc.

In summary, M&As studies suggest that the realization of operative synergies requires similar organizational contexts (especially similar management systems) in addition to resource relatedness (Björkman & Welch, 2015; Knoll, 2008; Larsson & Finkelstein, 1999). Furthermore, management style similarity may have its greatest effect on eventual synergy realization through its attenuation of cultural differences between merging organizations. Interestingly, many practitioners and consultants have argued that the difficulty companies have been having with synergy is due to a lack of managerial sophistication, as Campbell and Goold (1998) reveal. In the same vein, Desai et al. (n.d.) and Rosinski (2003) highlight that companies should take efforts to create a framework including mutually agreeable intercultural aspects of understanding to act as guidelines for post-merger synergy.

These findings reveal that, although most of the researchers point to the importance of intercultural synergy in M&A, in many cases there is not an appropriate practical approach. It can be stated that M&A research has underestimated the role of cultural integration. It should be also pointed out the intercultural synergy importance in determining the acceptable level of integration within a company.

4.3. What Is the Correlation between Intercultural Synergy and M&A Performance?

The management of the post-merger integration stage is probable to determine the extent to which intercultural synergy is realized. Strategic and financial decisions by management need to be considered concurrently with the role of the individual in the implementation activity to achieve the anticipated M&A performance. In a more general approach, Larsson and Finkelstein (1999) and Weber, Drori and Tarba (2012) remark that it is possible to integrate the combination, integration, employee, and performance issues into a comprehensive model that views M&A performance (conceptualized as synergy creation) as a function of combination potential, organizational integration, and employee resistance. Moreover, the performance of M&As depends not only on the synergy potential available before and during the merger but also on whether the synergy can actually be realised in the post-acquisition phase. In other words, M&A research must address both macro and micro levels.

Some scholars argue that although a significant amount of research has explored the patterns of M&As, the combined effects of national culture, corporate culture, and synergy potential on various integration approaches, as well as their influence on M&A performance, have never been simultaneously investigated and, in particular, what determines why some cross-border M&As are expected to result in higher synergies when compared to others (Sonenshine & Reynolds, 2014; Weber et al., 2011). There is a variety of meanings M&A scholars and practitioners attach to the M&A performance concept but it is not possible to talk about this concept as if it was a universal construct. For example, Chatterjee (1986) and Garzella and Fiorentino (2014) point out that performance measurement systems require the assessment of strategic factors affecting the value of synergy, because the value created by a merger is associated with one or more types of synergies.

Collusion-based synergistic mergers exert a positive externality on rival firm profitability. The negative impacts on acquired firm performance may not translate to weaker performance of the acquirer (Clougherty & Duso, 2011; Reus, Lamont & Ellis, 2015). Furthermore, it is also important to look at the positive synergies from the cultural differences, such as those of diversification, knowledge transfer and improved managerial quality, advantages in finding a path to a successful M&A as Warter and Warter (2015c) argue.

While most research up till now has evaluated M&A performance by examining abnormal stock returns or accounting profitability over a specific post-M&A window, Huyghebaert and Luypaert (2013) and Rosinski (2003) embrace a more comprehensive approach by disentangling the various sources of synergistic gains and taking into account that exploring all aspects of a culture is beyond our reach. In this regard, Basuil and Datta (2015) and Harris (2004) remark that with the increasing numbers of mergers and acquisitions, executives need to plan for the melding of different organizational cultures. In essence, a synergistic organizational culture is patiently developed. Furthermore, the outcomes of acquisition experience on acquisition performance are contingent on the level of cultural comparability between the acquiring and acquired firm countries, with the benefits of prior experience being greater in acquisitions undertaken in culturally similar countries.

In a couple of intriguing articles (Desai et al., n.d.; Richter et al., 2016) is stated that heavy emphasis on merger and acquisition technical issues may occur because they are generally more concrete and quantifiable. Thereby, managers may feel more comfortable focusing on these issues rather than cultural issues, which are more difficult to effectively measure in quantitative terms. Moreover, if research is focused on testing culture's impact, the measurement of culture should be based on cultural archetypes. Studies analysing the synergy realization in M&As (e.g., Cicon et al., 2014; Larsson & Finkelstein, 1999) have found that various sources of synergy define a combination's potential, which in turn is expected to affect the extent to which synergies will be realized in a merger or acquisition. Consequently, one would expect positive earnings surprises in the post-merger phase for those acquirers with high projected levels of synergy.

Blackard and Gibson (2002) and Shenkar (2012), for example, claim that cultural differences may be complementary and hence have a positive synergetic effect on investment and performance. To phrase it differently, under some circumstances, a disagreement can create synergy, aid in problem solving, and make the new merged firm more valuable. In the same direction, DePamphilis (2014) and Harris (2004) remark that cultural differences can instill creativity in the new corporation or create a contentious environment. The authors consider that whenever a company acquires or merges with another entity domestically or internationally, synergy skill is required. In sum, the presence of synergy is as an important determinant of value creation in a merger (Warter & Warter, 2015f). A similar point of view is presented by Rongxing (2012). He points out that the diversity of cultures can enable intercultural trade become a source of creativity and potential profitability.

In their conceptual article, Teerikangas and Very (2012) show that research into the culture-performance relationship paints an increasingly nuanced, yet continuously mixed, picture of the ways in which cultural differences, be they at organizational and/or at national levels exert both positive and negative impacts on the performance of M&A. The authors considered that several questions remain unanswered. For one, what is M&A performance against which culture can be measured? Should performance be measured in terms of financial or non-financial metrics; over what time frame following the deal? For another, who are the respondents, and how does the choice of buying or target firm respondents affect results? Are there industry effects, or country effects?

The overwhelming number of empirical studies measuring M&A performance is justified by the ambiguity of this concept with a lack of consensus on how to measure it. A great number of the reviewed articles conclude that the success of a merger or acquisition is determined by the degree of synergy realization. Most of the scholars and practitioners conclude that the lack of understanding of the nature and sources of synergy, especially the intercultural synergy is a source of M&As underperformance. Many scholars consider intercultural synergy realisation is a complex process, difficult to effectively measure while some scholars consider that the valuation is related to the area of headcount reduction.

For some scholars the cultural synergy is created by similarities in organisations but in the same time by differences. This tendency can be understood if we consider other authors' observations. They remark that empirical studies provide mixed results: some of them show that the intercultural synergy is highly significant after the merger while other studies show an insignificant effect on firm's performance or even a negative impact. The findings regarding the cross-cultural integration aspects are contradictory and the relation between M&A performance and intercultural synergy has remained unclear.

It must be noted that intercultural synergy is an important and controversial aspect of cross border M&As and the inconsistent results of previous studies require further research.

Chapter 5

Research Approach

5.1. Methodological Matters

The primary goal of the research was to uncover intercultural issues that managers encountered during the post-investment phase and they should have discovered during the pre-investment phase. The premise is that this stage of M&A is strongly influenced by intercultural synergy. This premise is based on the conducted literature review and the author's personal experience as practitioner.

The present study implied a consideration of both national and organizational culture as a factor to maximize the intercultural synergy.

A quantitative descriptive approach was used, using questionnaires to examine managers' perceptual evaluations of cultural differences and merger/acquisition outcomes.

The most appropriate way of data collection for this study was to develop questionnaires. Archive documents were definitely useful to reach the research goals. Also, direct observation was useful from author's previous experience as business consultant implied in M&A.

The data collection process was in absence of an interviewer and was done remotely, mainly by e-mail.

The study used well-defined research questions to generate numerical data, obtained by converting the levels of perception using the Likert scale.

The cross-sectional survey design was considered the most appropriate for this study. The survey activity was conducted to make it easy for respondents to answer and to get as much response, by ensuring a coherent communication strategy.

The population of this study consisted of managers from different countries who experienced first-hand the M&As and post-investment intercultural integration processes. It was used snowball sampling.

Close-ended questions allowed shortening the time of filling the questionnaire and, thus, obtaining higher response rates and to avoid poor-quality responses.

The target of the survey was cross-border M&A. Managers' perceptual evaluations of cultural differences were considered.

Databases of research institutes, local statistics offices and other international organizations were included as a guide of the data collection process. Other documents such as annual reports, policy and procedures manuals, and any public documents or such as press releases, stockholder presentations, manager presentations, government reports, web-sites, logs, statistical collections and newspaper accounts were also included as a guide of the data collection process.

This study attempts to explain M&A outcomes in terms of the impact that cultural differences have on the post-merger integration process.

This book aimed to answer some general questions regarding the influence of culture on the integration of the two companies, the extent of companies' integration, specific behavioural patterns, intentions, perceptions and attitudes of the managers associated with M&A's success, the relationship between the cultural orientation of the managers and their beliefs about factors influencing successful M&A, their expectations about the benefits and their management practices.

The specific questions of this research are: (1) Do the cultural differences lead to synergy effects?; (2) Do the cultural differences influence M&A's outcomes?; (3) Does the cultural specificity affect the perception on the M&A integration process and outcome?

The cultural specificity is not considered exclusively an effect of the national culture of the respondent. The respondents are identified culturally by the following categories: native language, country of origin, gender, profession, level of education, job level, and foreign languages.

The independent variables, presented in Table 1, are the national/organizational cultural characteristics and the attributes of the respondents. In order to have more edifying results, the countries were grouped in Cultural Clusters.

Table 1. Independent variables

No.	Independent Variable
1	Organizational functions and core values before the merger/acquisition
2	Cultural differences and respect in own company
3	Cultural differences and respect in the other company
4	Group identification in own company
5	Group identification in the other company
6	Agility in own company
7	Agility in the other company
8	Culture Cluster
9	Total number of languages
10	Number of foreign languages
11	Level of education
12	Job level
13	Profession

The dependent variables, presented in Table 2, are managers' M&A integration and outcome satisfaction in general and within particular facets and the perception on cultural differences.

The dependent variables are aggregation of the following individual attributes:

- Perception on intercultural synergy realization
- Perception of success/failure of merger/acquisition
- Perception on post-M&A conflict/cooperation between the teams of top managers
- Perceived cultural problems in integration

Table 2. Dependent variables

No.	Dependent Variable
1	Organizational functions and core values in the post-investment stage
2	Organizational functions in the post-investment stage
3	Organizational reliability in the other company
4	Organizational reliability in own company
5	Future insecurity in own company
6	Future insecurity in the other company
7	Resistance barriers in the other company
8	Resistance barriers in own company
9	Organizational distrust in the other company
10	Organizational distrust in own company
11	Intercultural competence
12	Conflict prevention
13	New culture
14	New practices
15	Intercultural synergy based decisions
16	National culture, importance for a cross border M&A
17	Organizational culture, importance for a cross border M&A
18	Professional culture, importance for a cross border M&A
19	Managers' degree of autonomy, impact on M&A outcome
20	Organizational change resistance, impact on top management's decisions
21	Top management's decisions, impact on the integration process outcome
22	Top management's actions, impact on M&A success
23	Integration outcome
24	M&A outcome
25	National culture, impact on the success/failure of the M&A process
26	Organizational culture, impact on the success/failure of the M&A process
27	Professional culture, impact on the success/failure of the M&A process
28	Profit of own company change estimation
29	Profit of the other company change estimation
30	Sales of own company change estimation
31	Sales of the other company change estimation
32	Market share of own company change estimation
33	Market share of the other company change estimation
34	Return on equity (ROE) of own company change estimation
35	Return on equity (ROE) of the other company change estimation
36	Return on assets (ROA) of own company change estimation
37	Return on assets (ROA) of the other company change estimation

- Expectations regarding the change of financial indicators after the merger/acquisition
- Turnover of the top managers
- Perception on cultural differences before and after the merger/acquisition in companies' functions
- Perception on cultural features of the two companies before and after the merger/acquisition
- Skills or abilities perceived as useful in the post-M&A stage

The structure of the questionnaire is presented below:

- M&A experience
- Cultural Differences (Intercultural Synergy)
- Outcome of the Merger/Acquisition
- Background of the Respondent

The survey instrument focused on four directions: demographics, belief, practices and perception. The questionnaire intended to get data about: perception on intercultural synergy realization, perception on post-M&A conflict/cooperation between the teams of top managers, perception of success/failure of merger/acquisition, perceived cultural problems in integration, expectations regarding the change of financial indicators after the merger/acquisition, turnover of the top managers, perception on cultural differences before and after the merger/acquisition in companies' functions, perception on cultural features of the two companies before and after the merger/acquisition and skills or abilities perceived as useful in the post-M&A stage. The questions were prepared taking into account the utility of collected responses, the probability of getting the expected data and the willingness of the respondents to answer precisely the questions.

The questionnaire is presented in the Appendix.

5.2. Data Collection

The data was based on one data collection round.
Selection was based on the following criteria:

- The acquired company or one of the parties in merger or acquisition was a local firm (company) from the selected countries.
- The minimum turnover of the two parties involved exceeded EUR 1 million.
- The acquiring party had gained a majority stake (over 50%) of the acquired firm (only in case of acquisitions).
- Management buy-outs and purely financial acquisitions were excluded.

The participants were top managers and consultants who experienced first-hand the M&As and post-investment intercultural integration processes. Their participation was anonymous to each other in order to express without restraint their beliefs and perceptions.

The questionnaire included closed questions regarding the intercultural problems they and their organization experienced during the post-investment integration phase in M&As with respect to national, organizational and professional cultural implications.

Participation in the research was requested through direct and indirect channels to potential participants who had the above mentioned profile.. Channels included:

1. Friends and colleagues, both practitioners and scholars.
2. Referrals from friends and colleagues.
3. Emails to members of M&A communities of interest.
4. Postings on M&A web forums, web sites and electronic distribution lists.
5. Email referrals from people who filled the online questionnaire.

Data collection was done by inviting the participants to submit their filled questionnaires by email. To obtain high quality responses, the top managers and consultants were contacted before sending out the questionnaire. This was done via telephone or by e-mail. The timeline allowed a maximum of eight weeks for replies. A follow-up to the original request for participation e-mail was prepared for mailing and sent to any of the managers and consultants who had not replied within the eight-week time frame. In addition, other channels such as social networking sites for scholars and practitioners were used: Research Gate, LinkedIn, Academia.edu, Facebook.

Each participant answered based on the lived experiences from their perspective. To get a cohesive understanding on how some of the individual experiences tied together, participants were selected from both acquired and acquiring companies.

Statistical analyses were conducted using SPSS 20.0.

To drill the complex intercultural facets during the post-investment integration phase and to understand the lived experience of the participants, a preliminary analysis of data was performed.

Data Analysis begins with an analysis on the profile of the respondents and the background of their companies. It also shows demographic data of the respondents.

Factor Analysis helped the extraction of 19 factors structured in 9 groups (dimensions), as shown in Chapter 6.

The dimensions and the corresponding factors are presented in Table 3.

General linear model was used in some of the cases because the analyses include both numeric (interval level) and categorical variables (nominal level). The other dependencies were studied using statistical regression.

Table 4 shows the checked dependencies between the dependent and the independent variables. It also indicates the statistical method used. After applying the Levene (for GLM) test and checking the p- values (for Regression), a part of the dependencies were eliminated from further processing. Table 5 presents the processed dependencies between the dependent and the independent variables.

Table 3. Dimensions, factors and basic items

No.	Group	Factor	Basic item
1.	Cultural differences between the companies before the merger/acquisition	Organizational functions and core values	Management
			Company values and practices
			Finance
			Production
			Human resource management
2.	Culture of own company before the merger/acquisition	Cultural differences and respect	Contains few different cultural groups
			Low level of valuing cultural differences
			Low tolerance of cultural differences
			Uniculturalism
		Group identification	Very strong belief in own competitiveness
			Strong identity
			Strong sense of belonging together
		Agility	No readiness for change
			Low level of flexibility
			Low level of creativity
3.	Culture of the other company before the merger/acquisition	Cultural differences and respect	Contains few different cultural groups
			Low level of valuing cultural differences
			Low tolerance of cultural differences
			Uniculturalism
		Group identification	Very strong belief in own competitiveness
			Strong identity
			Strong sense of belonging together
		Agility	No readiness for change
			Low level of flexibility
			Low level of creativity
4.	Cultural differences between the companies in the post-investment stage	Organizational functions and core values	Management
			Company values and practices
			Finance
			Production
			Human resource management
5.	Synergistic effects achieved by the integration of different areas	Organizational functions	Management
			Finance
			Production
			Human resource management
6.	Organizational problems in own company as result of the merger/acquisition	Future insecurity	Uncertainty about the future
			Divergent goals and objectives
			Lack of motivation
		Organizational reliability	Poor coordination/integration
			Low professional trust

No.	Group	Factor	Basic item
			Poor communication
			Poor integration leadership
			Low organizational identification
		Organizational distrust	Mistrust in rewards system
			Mistrust in advancement opportunities
			Loss of key persons
		Resistance barriers	Low intercultural synergy
			Increase in absenteeism
			Resistance to change
			Sabotage
7.	Organizational problems in the other company as result of the merger/ acquisition	Future insecurity	Uncertainty about the future
			Divergent goals and objectives
			Lack of motivation
		Organizational reliability	Poor coordination/integration
			Low professional trust
			Poor communication
			Poor integration leadership
			Low organizational identification
		Organizational distrust	Mistrust in rewards system
			Mistrust in advancement opportunities
			Loss of key persons
		Resistance barriers	Low intercultural synergy
			Increase in absenteeism
			Resistance to change
			Sabotage
8.	Problems in cooperation between the two teams of top managers	Conflict prevention	Misunderstandings
			Mistrust
			Incapacity to reconcile different points of view
			Unwillingness to reconcile different points of view
			Conflicts
9.	Skills/abilities useful in the post-investment stage	Intercultural competence	Cultural differences understanding
			Multilingualism
			Adaptation to a different culture
			Awareness of own culture
			Respect for otherness
			Communicative awareness
			Behavioral flexibility
			Readiness for change

Table 4. Checked dependencies between dependent and independent variables

No.	Dependent variable	Independent variable	Statistic type
1.	Organizational functions and core values in the post-investment stage	Organizational functions and core values before the merger/acquisition	Regression
2.	Organizational functions in the post-investment stage	Cultural differences and respect in own company	Regression
		Cultural differences and respect in the other company	
3.	Organizational functions in the post-investment stage	Group identification in own company	Regression
		Group identification in the other company	
4.	Organizational functions in the post-investment stage	Agility in own company	Regression
		Agility in the other company	
5.	Organizational reliability in the other company	Cultural differences and respect in own company	Regression
		Cultural differences and respect in the other company	
6.	Organizational reliability in the other company	Group identification in own company	Regression
		Group identification in the other company	
7.	Organizational reliability in the other company	Agility in own company	Regression
		Agility in the other company	
8.	Organizational reliability in own company	Cultural differences and respect in own company	Regression
		Cultural differences and respect in the other company	
9.	Organizational reliability in own company	Group identification in own company	Regression
		Group identification in the other company	
10.	Organizational reliability in own company	Agility in own company	Regression
		Agility in the other company	
11.	Future insecurity in own company	Cultural differences and respect in own company	Regression
		Cultural differences and respect in the other company	
12.	Future insecurity in own company	Group identification in own company	Regression
		Group identification in the other company	

No.	Dependent variable	Independent variable	Statistic type
13.	Future insecurity in own company	Agility in own company	Regression
		Agility in the other company	
14.	Future insecurity in the other company	Cultural differences and respect in own company	Regression
		Cultural differences and respect in the other company	
15.	Future insecurity in the other company	Group identification in own company	Regression
		Group identification in the other company	
16.	Future insecurity in the other company	Agility in own company	Regression
		Agility in the other company	
17.	Resistance barriers in the other company	Cultural differences and respect in own company	Regression
		Cultural differences and respect in the other company	
18.	Resistance barriers in the other company	Group identification in own company	Regression
		Group identification in the other company	
19.	Resistance barriers in the other company	Agility in own company	Regression
		Agility in the other company	
20.	Resistance barriers in own company	Cultural differences and respect in own company	Regression
		Cultural differences and respect in the other company	
21.	Resistance barriers in own company	Group identification in own company	Regression
		Group identification in the other company	
22.	Resistance barriers in own company	Agility in own company	Regression
		Agility	
23.	Organizational distrust in the other company	Cultural differences and respect in own company	Regression
		Cultural differences and respect in the other company	
24.	Organizational distrust in the other company	Group identification in own company	Regression
		Group identification in the other company	
25.	Organizational distrust in the other company	Agility in own company	Regression
		Agility in the other company	

Table 4. (Continued)

No.	Dependent variable	Independent variable	Statistic type
26.	Organizational distrust in own company	Cultural differences and respect in own company	Regression
		Cultural differences and respect in the other company	
27.	Organizational distrust in own company	Group identification in own company	Regression
		Group identification in the other company	
28.	Organizational distrust in own company	Agility in own company	Regression
		Agility in the other company	
29.	Intercultural competence	Culture Cluster	GLM
		Total number of languages	
30.	Conflict prevention	Culture Cluster	GLM
		Level of education	
31.	New culture	Cultural differences and respect in own company	Regression
		Cultural differences and respect in the other company	
32.	New practices	Group identification in own company	Regression
		Group identification in the other company	
33.	Intercultural synergy based decisions	Cultural differences and respect in own company	Regression
		Cultural differences and respect in the other company	
34.	National culture, importance for a cross border M&A	Culture Cluster	GLM
		Number of foreign languages	
35.	Organizational culture, importance for a cross border M&A	Culture Cluster	GLM
		Job level	
36.	Professional culture, importance for a cross border M&A	Culture Cluster	GLM
		Profession	
37.	Managers' degree of autonomy, impact on M&A outcome	Agility in own company	Regression
		Agility in the other company	

No.	Dependent variable	Independent variable	Statistic type
38.	Organizational change resistance, impact on top management's decisions	Agility in own company	Regression
		Agility in the other company	
39.	Top management's decisions, impact on the integration process outcome	Cultural differences and respect in own company	Regression
		Cultural differences and respect in the other company	
40.	Top management's actions, impact on M&A success	Culture Cluster	GLM
		Profession	
41.	Integration outcome	Cultural differences and respect in own company	Regression
		Cultural differences and respect	
42.	M&A outcome	Cultural differences and respect in own company	Regression
		Cultural differences and respect in the other company	
43.	National culture, impact on the success/failure of the M&A process	Culture Cluster	GLM
		Total number of languages	
44.	Organizational culture, impact on the success/failure of the M&A process	Culture Cluster	GLM
		Level of education	
45.	Professional culture, impact on the success/failure of the M&A process	Culture Cluster	GLM
		Profession	
46.	Profit of own company change estimation	Culture Cluster	GLM
		Profession	
47.	Profit of the other company change estimation	Culture Cluster	GLM
		Profession	
48.	Sales of own company change estimation	Culture Cluster	GLM
		Level of education	
49.	Sales of the other company change estimation	Culture Cluster	GLM
		Level of education	
50.	Market share of own company change estimation	Culture Cluster	GLM
		Profession	
51.	Market share of the other company change estimation	Culture Cluster	GLM
		Profession	
52.	Return on equity (ROE) of own company change estimation	Culture Cluster	GLM
		Level of education	

Table 4. (Continued)

No.	Dependent variable	Independent variable	Statistic type
53.	Return on equity (ROE) of the other company change estimation	Culture Cluster	GLM
		Level of education	
54.	Return on assets (ROA) of own company change estimation	Culture Cluster	GLM
		Job level	
55.	Return on assets (ROA) of the other company change estimation	Culture Cluster	GLM
		Job level	

Table 5. Processed dependencies between dependent and independent variables

No.	Dependent variable	Independent variable	Statistic type	Research Question
1.	Organizational functions and core values in the post-investment stage	Organizational functions and core values before the merger/acquisition	Regression	1
2.	Organizational functions in the post-investment stage	Cultural differences and respect in own company	Regression	1
		Cultural differences and respect in the other company		
3.	Organizational functions in the post-investment stage	Group identification in own company	Regression	1
		Group identification in the other company		
4.	Organizational functions in the post-investment stage	Agility in own company	Regression	1
		Agility in the other company		
5.	Organizational reliability in the other company	Agility in own company	Regression	2
		Agility in the other company		
6.	Organizational reliability in own company	Agility in own company	Regression	2
		Agility in the other company		
7.	Future insecurity in own company	Cultural differences and respect in own company	Regression	2
		Cultural differences and respect in the other company		

No.	Dependent variable	Independent variable	Statistic type	Research Question
8.	Future insecurity in the other company	Cultural differences and respect in own company	Regression	2
		Cultural differences and respect in the other company		
9.	Resistance barriers in the other company	Group identification in own company	Regression	2
		Group identification in the other company		
10.	Resistance barriers in own company	Group identification in own company	Regression	2
		Group identification in the other company		
11.	Organizational distrust in the other company	Agility in own company	Regression	2
		Agility in the other company		
12.	Organizational distrust in own company	Agility in own company	Regression	2
		Agility in the other company		
13.	Intercultural competence	Culture Cluster	GLM	3
		Total number of languages		
14.	New culture	Cultural differences and respect in own company	Regression	1
		Cultural differences and respect in the other company		
15.	New practices	Group identification in own company	Regression	1
		Group identification in the other company		
16.	Intercultural synergy based decisions	Cultural differences and respect in own company	Regression	1
		Cultural differences and respect in the other company		
17.	Managers' degree of autonomy, impact on M&A outcome	Agility in own company	Regression	2
		Agility in the other company		
18.	Organizational change resistance, impact on top management's decisions	Agility in own company	Regression	2
		Agility in the other company		

Table 5. (Continued)

No.	Dependent variable	Independent variable	Statistic type	Research Question
19.	Top management's decisions, impact on the integration process outcome	Cultural differences and respect in own company	Regression	2
		Cultural differences and respect in the other company		
20.	Integration outcome	Cultural differences and respect in own company	Regression	2
		Cultural differences and respect in the other company		
21.	M&A outcome	Cultural differences and respect in own company	Regression	2
		Cultural differences and respect in the other company		
22.	Profit of own company change estimation	Culture Cluster	GLM	3
		Profession		
23.	Profit of the other company change estimation	Culture Cluster	GLM	3
		Profession		
24.	Sales of own company change estimation	Culture Cluster	GLM	3
		Level of education		
25.	Sales of the other company change estimation	Culture Cluster	GLM	3
		Level of education		
26.	Market share of the other company change estimation	Culture Cluster	GLM	3
		Profession		

Chapter 6

THE NINE DIMENSIONS MODEL OF THE POST-M&A STAGE

The category with the highest percent (40%) was the one in which the respondent company was involved in two M&As whilst only 16 percent of the sample referred to five M&As. Half of the respondents were part of two M&A deals and only 2% of the participants were part of four M&A deals.

Most of the respondents (28%) were involved in M&A deals smaller than 3 million EUR but also 22 percent of the sample was part of M&A deals bigger than 50 million EUR.

Most of the respondents (38%) participated on the acquired company side.

Most of the respondents (38%) considered the questionnaire clear enough and only 6 percent of them considered it not so clear.

10 percent of the respondents are two languages native speakers.

A small percent of the participants (4%) consider they have two countries of origin.

Most of the respondents (76%) speak English as first foreign language, followed by French and German in the same percent (6%).

Other respondents speak different foreign languages as first foreign language. For instance 6% of the respondents speak German as first foreign language.

Of the respondents, 90% have one native language and 10% have two native languages.

Most of the participants (40%) speak one foreign language, followed by 30 % of the respondents who speak two foreign languages. Only 4% of the respondents speak five foreign languages.

While 34% of the participants speak two languages, only 4 % of them speak six languages.

The profession of most of the participants (46%) is economist, but only 2% of the respondents are psychologists.

The category with the highest count (46%) is Master degree, while 20% of the participants hold a PhD.

Top managers represent 76 percent of the sample while middle managers represent only 8 percent of the sample.

It can be noticed that the respondents come from all the six cultural clusters defined based on Hofstede's first four dimensions. The culture clusters' concept is presented in Table 6. Table 7 presents examples of countries from all the culture clusters (Wursten, n.d.a; Wursten, n.d.b; Wursten and Lanzer, n.d.).

Most of the respondents come from the Pyramid cluster (46.0 %) followed by the Machine (24.0%) and Solar System (14.0%) clusters.

Table 6. Culture clusters' concept

Contest	**Network**	**Family**	**Pyramid**	**Solar System**	**Machine**
Competition	Consensus	Loyalty and hierarchy	Loyalty, hierarchy and implicit order	Hierarchy and impersonal bureaucracy	Order
-PDI +IDV -UAI +MAS	-PDI +IDV -UAI/±UAI -MAS	+PDI -IDV -UAI	+PDI -IDV +UAI	+PDI +IDV +UAI	-PDI ± IDV/+IDV +UAI

Table 7. Culture clusters examples

Contest	Great Britain, USA
Network	Netherlands, Sweden, Norway
Pyramid	France, Italy, Spain
Family	Morocco, Russia, Brazil
Solar System	China, Vietnam
Oil Machine	Germany, Austria

6.1. The Cultural Differences between the Companies before the Merger/Acquisition Dimension

The factors come from the questionnaire item below:

How would you describe the cultural differences between the companies before the merger/acquisition in the following areas?

Table 8 presents the factors and corresponding items for Cultural differences between the companies before the merger/acquisition.

Table 8. Factors and corresponding items for Cultural differences between the companies before the merger/acquisition

Item number	**Item name**	**Item code**	**Factor**	**Factor name**
Q 5.1.	Management	m	F1	Organizational functions and core values
Q 5.2.	Company values and practices	cvp	F1	Organizational functions and core values
Q 5.3.	Finance	f	F1	Organizational functions and core values
Q 5.4.	Production	p	F1	Organizational functions and core values
Q 5.5.	Human resource management	hrm	F1	Organizational functions and core values

In the KMO and Bartlett's Test results for Cultural differences between the companies before the merger/acquisition table, the value for the "Measure of Sampling Adequacy" is 0.799, and "Bartlett's Test of Sphericity" has an associated P value (Sig. in the table) less than 0.001. A valid factor analysis can be performed.

From the Total Variance Explained results for Cultural differences between the companies before the merger/acquisition table one component was extracted. The first component has eigenvalue over 1.00, that explain more than 58% of the total variability in the data. One factor formula is correct.

The unrotated factor loadings show high positive loadings on the first factor (Figure 1).

Human resource management, Management, Production, Company values and practices and Finance (Q 5.5, Q 5.1, Q 5.4, Q 5.2 and Q 5.3) all have high positive loadings on the factor.

It can be recognized the factor (F1) as "Organizational functions and core values."

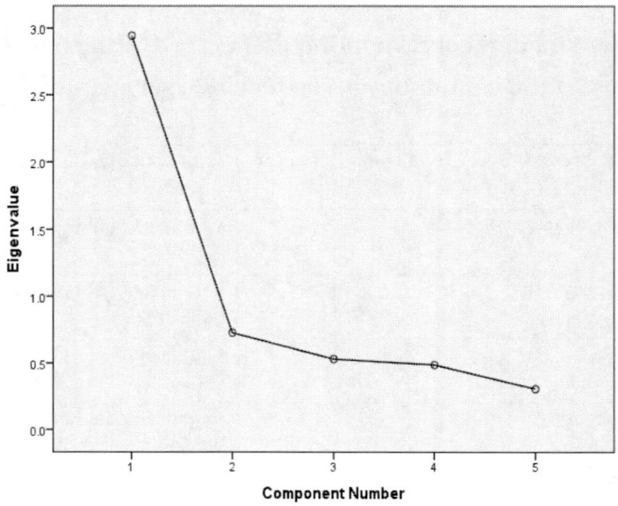

Figure 1. Scree plot for Cultural differences between the companies before the merger/acquisition.

There is a factor equation (Table 9):

F1 = 0.278* **m** + 0.244* **cvp** + 0.241***f** + 0.257* **p** + 0.281* **hrm** (1)

Table 9. Component Score Coefficient Matrix for Cultural differences between the companies before the merger/acquisition

Component Score Coefficient Matrix	
	Component
	1
Q 5.1	.278
Q 5.2	.244
Q 5.3	.241
Q 5.4	.257
Q 5.5	.281

6.2. The Culture of Own Company before the Merger/Acquisition Dimension

The factors come from the questionnaire item below:

How would you describe the culture of your company before the merger/acquisition?

Table 10 presents the factors and corresponding items for Culture of own company before the merger/acquisition.

In the KMO and Bartlett's Test results for Culture of own company before the merger/acquisition table the value for the “Measure of Sampling Adequacy” is 0.838, and “Bartlett’s Test of Sphericity” has an associated P value (Sig. in the table) less than 0.001. A valid factor analysis can be performed.

From the Total Variance Explained results for Culture of own company before the merger/acquisition table three components were extracted. The first three components have eigenvalues over 1.00, that explain more than 77% of the total variability in the data. Three factors formula is correct.

Table 10. Factors and corresponding items for Culture of own company before the merger/acquisition

Item number	Item name	Item code	Factor	Factor name
Q 7.1.	Contains few different cultural groups	dcg	F1	Cultural differences and respect
Q 7.2.	Low level of valuing cultural differences	vcd	F1	Cultural differences and respect
Q 7.3.	Low tolerance of cultural differences	tcd	F1	Cultural differences and respect
Q 7.4.	Uniculturalism	u	F1	Cultural differences and respect
Q 7.5.	Very strong belief in own competitiveness	boc	F2	Group identification
Q 7.6.	Strong identity	i	F2	Group identification
Q 7.7.	Strong sense of belonging together	sbt	F2	Group identification
Q 7.8.	No readiness for change	rc	F3	Agility
Q 7.9.	Low level of flexibility	f	F3	Agility
Q 7.10.	Low level of creativity	c	F3	Agility

The first factor of the initial solution is much more important than the second and the third. The eigenvalues of the rotated factor are 2.705, 2.630 and 2.391, compared to 4.136, 2.439 and 1.151 in the initial solution.

The unrotated factor loadings show high positive loadings on the first factor (Figure 2).

The three rotated factors are just as good as the initial factors in explaining and reproducing the observed correlation matrix. In the rotated factors table, Different cultural groups, Tolerance of cultural differences, Valuing cultural differences and Uniculturalism (Q 7.1, Q 7.3, Q 7.2 and Q 7.4) all have high positive loadings on the first factor, Sense of belonging together, Belief in own competitiveness and Identity (Q 7.7, Q 7.5 and Q 7.6) all have high positive loadings on the second factor, Flexibility, Creativity and Readiness for change (Q 7.9, Q 7.10 and Q 7.8) has high positive loadings on the third factor.

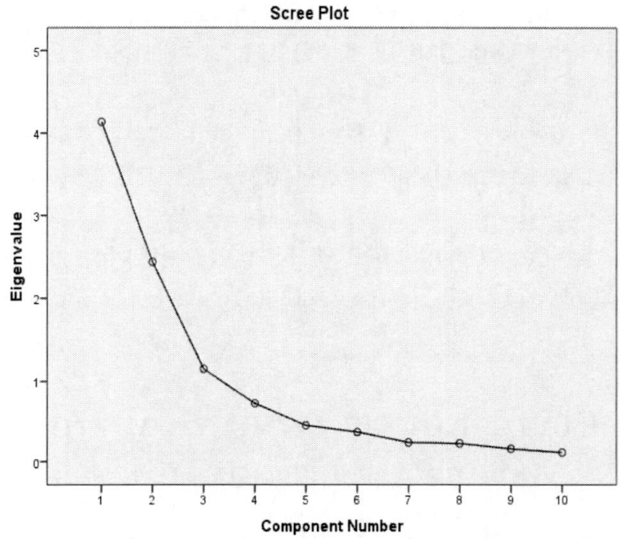

Figure 2. Scree plot for Culture of own company before the merger/acquisition.

Table 11. Component Score Coefficient Matrix for Culture of own company before the merger/acquisition

	Component		
	1	2	3
Q 7.1	.432	.129	-.155
Q 7.2	.356	.074	-.079
Q 7.3	.346	-.025	-.112
Q 7.4	.181	-.018	.144
Q 7.5	.034	.348	.004
Q 7.6	.045	.353	.033
Q 7.7	.126	.386	-.060
Q 7.8	-.019	.066	.267
Q 7.9	-.211	-.099	.490
Q 7.10	-.103	.012	.411

It can be recognized the first rotated factor (F1) as "Cultural differences and respect", the second rotated factor (F2) as "Group identification" and the third rotated factor (F3) as "Agility."

There are three factor equations (Table 11):

F1 = 0.432 * **dcg** + 0.356 * **vcd** + 0.346 * **tcd** + 0.181 * **u** + 0.034 * **boc** + 0.045 * **i** + 0.126 * **sbt** - 0.019 * **rc** - 0.211 * **f** - 0.103 * **c** (2)

F2 = 0.129 * **dcg** + 0.074 * **vcd** - 0.025 * **tcd** - 0.018 * **u** + 0.348 * **boc** + 0.353 * **i** + 0.386 * **sbt** + 0.066 * **rc** - 0.099 * **f** + 0.012 * **c** (3)

F3 = - 0.155 * **dcg** - 0.079 * **vcd** - 0.112 * **tcd** + 0.144 * **u** + 0.004 * **boc** + 0.033 * **i** - 0.060 * **sbt** + 0.267 * **rc** + 0.490 * **f** + 0.411 * **c** (4)

6.3. The Culture of the Other Company before the Merger/Acquisition Dimension

The factors come from the questionnaire item below:

How would you describe the culture of the other company before the merger/acquisition?

Table 12 presents the factors and corresponding items for Culture of the other company before the merger/acquisition.

In the KMO and Bartlett's Test results for Culture of the other company before the merger/acquisition table the value for the "Measure of Sampling Adequacy" is 0.751, and "Bartlett's Test of Sphericity" has an associated P value (Sig. in the table) less than 0.001. A valid factor analysis can be performed.

From the Total Variance Explained results for Culture of the other company before the merger/acquisition can be noticed that 3 components were extracted. The first three components have eigenvalues over 1.00, that explain more than 77% of the total variability in the data. Three factors formula is correct.

The first factor of the initial solution is much more important than the second and the third. The eigenvalues of the rotated factor are 3.054, 2.363 and 2.306, compared to 4.043, 2.288 and 1.393 in the initial solution.

The unrotated factor loadings show high positive loadings on the first factor (Figure 3).

Table 12. Factors and corresponding items for Culture of the other company before the merger/acquisition

Item number	Item name	Item code	Factor	Factor name
Q 8.1.	Contains few different cultural groups	dcg	F1	Cultural differences and respect
Q 8.2.	Low level of valuing cultural differences	vcd	F1	Cultural differences and respect
Q 8.3.	Low tolerance of cultural differences	tcd	F1	Cultural differences and respect
Q 8.4.	Uniculturalism	u	F1	Cultural differences and respect
Q 8.5.	Very strong belief in own competitiveness	boc	F3	Group identification
Q 8.6.	Strong identity	i	F3	Group identification
Q 8.7.	Strong sense of belonging together	sbt	F3	Group identification
Q 8.8.	No readiness for change	rc	F2	Agility
Q 8.9.	Low level of flexibility	f	F2	Agility
Q 8.10.	Low level of creativity	c	F2	Agility

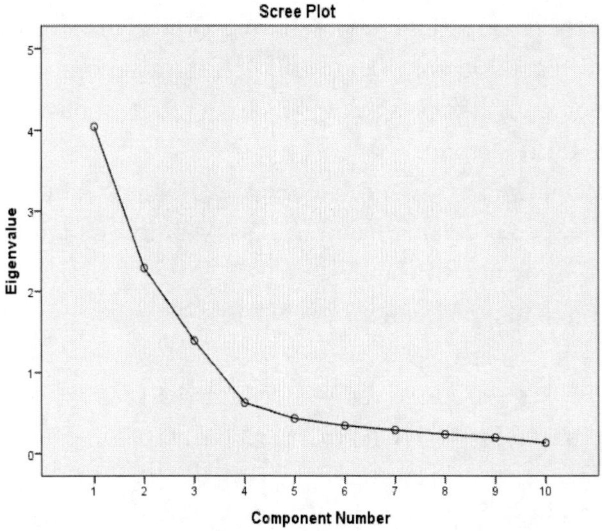

Figure 3. Scree plot for Culture of the other company before the merger/acquisition.

Table 13. Component Score Coefficient Matrix for Culture of the other company before the merger/acquisition

	Component		
	1	2	3
Q 8.1	.358	-.169	-.028
Q 8.2	.318	-.071	-.057
Q 8.3	.200	.047	.089
Q 8.4	.327	-.076	-.032
Q 8.5	-.041	-.018	.374
Q 8.6	-.057	.040	.415
Q 8.7	.028	-.016	.338
Q 8.8	-.048	.360	.016
Q 8.9	-.193	.489	-.003
Q 8.10	-.028	.357	-.018

The three rotated factors are just as good as the initial factors in explaining and reproducing the observed correlation matrix. In the rotated factors table, Uniculturalism, Different cultural groups, Valuing cultural differences and Tolerance of cultural differences (Q 8.4, Q 8.1, Q 8.2 and Q 8.3) all have high positive loadings on the first factor, Flexibility, Creativity and Readiness for change (Q 8.9, Q 8.10 and Q 8.8) all have high positive loadings on the second factor, Identity, Belief in own competitiveness and Sense of belonging together (Q 8.6, Q 8.5 and Q 8.7) all have high positive loadings on the third factor.

It can be recognized the first rotated factor (F1) as "Cultural differences and respect", the second rotated factor (F2) as "Agility" and the third rotated factor (F3) as "Group identification".

There are three factor equations (Table 13):

$$\mathbf{F1} = 0.358 * \mathbf{dcg} + 0.318 * \mathbf{vcd} + 0.200 * \mathbf{tcd} + 0.327 * \mathbf{u} - 0.041 * \mathbf{boc} - 0.057 * \mathbf{i} + 0.028 * \mathbf{sbt} - 0.048 * \mathbf{rc} - 0.193 * \mathbf{f} - 0.028 * \mathbf{c} \quad (5)$$

$$\mathbf{F2} = - 0.169 * \mathbf{dcg} - 0.071 * \mathbf{vcd} + 0.047 * \mathbf{tcd} - 0.076 * \mathbf{u} - 0.018 * \mathbf{boc} + 0.040 * \mathbf{i} - 0.016 * \mathbf{sbt} + 0.360 * \mathbf{rc} + 0.489 * \mathbf{f} + 0.357 * \mathbf{c} \quad (6)$$

$$\mathbf{F3} = -0.028 * \mathbf{dcg} - 0.057 * \mathbf{vcd} + 0.089 * \mathbf{tcd} - 0.032 * \mathbf{u} + 0.374 * \mathbf{boc} + 0.415 * \mathbf{i} + 0.338 * \mathbf{sbt} + 0.016 * \mathbf{rc} - 0.003 * \mathbf{f} - 0.018 * \mathbf{c} \quad (7)$$

6.4. The Cultural Differences between the Companies in the Post-Investment Stage Dimension

The factors come from the questionnaire item below:

How would you describe the cultural differences between the companies in the post-investment stage in the following areas?

Table 14 presents the factors and corresponding items for Cultural differences between the companies in the post-investment stage.

In the KMO and Bartlett's Test results for Cultural differences between the companies in the post-investment stage table the value for the "Measure of Sampling Adequacy" is 0.804, and "Bartlett's Test of Sphericity" has an associated P value (Sig. in the table) less than 0.001. A valid factor analysis can be performed.

Table 14. Factors and corresponding items for Cultural differences between the companies in the post-investment stage

Item number	Item name	Item code	Factor	Factor name
Q 6.1.	Management	m	F1	Organizational functions and core values
Q 6.2.	Company values and practices	cvp	F1	Organizational functions and core values
Q 6.3.	Finance	f	F1	Organizational functions and core values
Q 6.4.	Production	p	F1	Organizational functions and core values
Q 6.5.	Human resource management	hrm	F1	Organizational functions and core values

From the Total Variance Explained results for Cultural differences between the companies in the post-investment stage table one component was extracted. The first component has eigenvalue over 1.00, that explain more than 67% of the total variability in the data. One factor formula is correct.

The unrotated factor loadings show high positive loadings on the first factor (Figure 4).

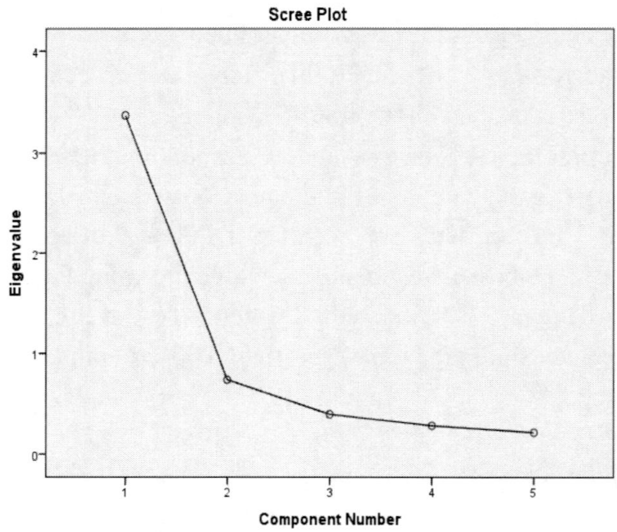

Figure 4. Scree plot for Cultural differences between the companies in the post-investment stage.

Human resource management, Finance, Production, Company values and practices and Management (Q 6.5, Q 6.3, Q 6.4, Q 6.2 and Q 6.1) all have high positive loadings on the factor.

It can be recognized the factor (F1) as "Organizational functions and core values".

There is a factor equation (Table 15):

$$\mathbf{F1} = 0.230 * \mathbf{m} + 0.233 * \mathbf{cvp} + 0.254 * \mathbf{f} + 0.236 * \mathbf{p} + 0.274 * \mathbf{hrm} \quad (8)$$

Table 15. Component Score Coefficient Matrix for for Cultural differences between the companies in the post-investment stage

	Component
	1
Q 6.1	.230
Q 6.2	.233
Q 6.3	.254
Q 6.4	.236
Q 6.5	.264

6.5. The Synergistic Effects Achieved by the Integration of Different Areas Dimension

The factors come from the questionnaire item below:

When evaluating the post-investment stage, have synergistic effects been achieved by the integration of different areas?

Table 16 presents the factors and corresponding items for Synergistic effects achieved by the integration of different areas.

In the KMO and Bartlett's Test results for Synergistic effects achieved by the integration of different areas table the value for the "Measure of Sampling Adequacy" is 0.734, and "Bartlett's Test of Sphericity" has an associated P value (Sig. in the table) less than 0.001. A valid factor analysis can be performed.

Table 16. Factors and corresponding items for Synergistic effects achieved by the integration of different areas

Item number	Item name	Item code	Factor	Factor name
Q 22.1.	Management	m	F1	Organizational functions
Q 22.2.	Finance	f	F1	Organizational functions
Q 22.3.	Production	p	F1	Organizational functions
Q 22.4.	Human resource management	hrm	F1	Organizational functions

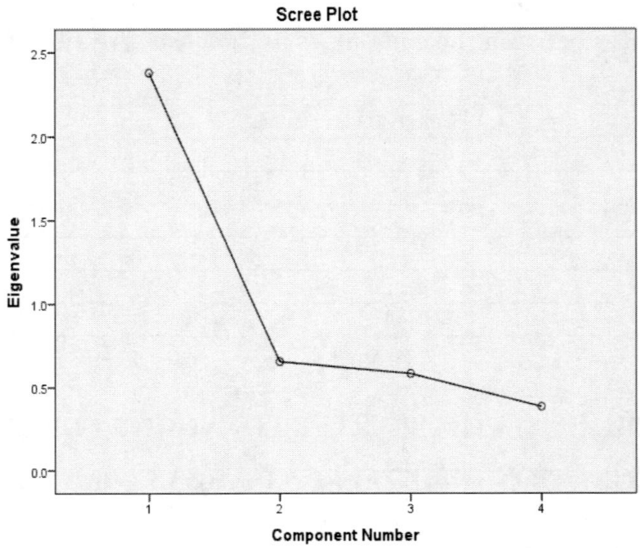

Figure 5. Scree plot for Synergistic effects achieved by the integration of different areas.

From the Total Variance Explained results for Synergistic effects achieved by the integration of different areas table one component was extracted. The first component has eigenvalue over 1.00, that explain more than 59% of the total variability in the data. One factor formula is correct.

The unrotated factor loadings show high positive loadings on the first factor (Figure 5).

Table 17. Component Score Coefficient Matrix for Synergistic effects achieved by the integration of different areas

	Component
	1
Q 22.1	.342
Q 22.2	.316
Q 22.3	.309
Q 22.4	.328

Management, Human resource management, Finance and Production (Q 22.1, Q 22.4, Q 22.2 and Q 22.3) all have high positive loadings on the factor.

It can be recognized the factor (F1) as "Organizational functions".

There is a factor equation (Table 17):

$$\mathbf{F1} = 0.342 * \mathbf{m} + 0.316 * \mathbf{f} + 0.309 * \mathbf{p} + 0.328 * \mathbf{hrm} \quad (9)$$

6.6. The Organizational Problems in Own Company as Result of the Merger/Acquisition Dimension

The factors come from the questionnaire item below:

As a result of the merger/acquisition, have there been following organizational problems in your company?

Table 18 presents the factors and corresponding items for Organizational problems in own company as result of the merger/ acquisition.

In the KMO and Bartlett's Test results for Organizational problems in own company as result of the merger/acquisition table the value for the "Measure of Sampling Adequacy" is 0.729, and "Bartlett's Test of Sphericity" has an associated P value (Sig. in the table) less than 0.001. A valid factor analysis can be performed.

From the total Variance Explained results for Organizational problems in own company as result of the merger/acquisition table four components were extracted. The first four components have eigenvalues over 1.00, that explain more than 72% of the total variability in the data. Four factors formula is correct. The first factor of the initial solution is much more important than the second, the third and the fourth. The eigenvalues of the rotated factor are 3.974, 2.490, 2.390 and 1.993, compared to 6.417, 1.741, 1.466 and 1.223 in the initial solution.

Table 18. Factors and corresponding items for Organizational problems in own company as result of the merger/acquisition

Item number	Item name	Item code	Factor	Factor name
Q 18.1.	Uncertainty about the future	uaf	F2	Future insecurity
Q 18.2.	Divergent goals and objectives	go	F2	Future insecurity
Q 18.3.	Poor coordination/integration	ci	F1	Organizational reliability
Q 18.4.	Low professional trust	pt	F1	Organizational reliability
Q 18.5.	Mistrust in rewards system	mrs	F4	Organizational distrust
Q 18.6.	Mistrust in advancement opportunities	mao	F4	Organizational distrust
Q 18.7.	Poor communication	c	F1	Organizational reliability
Q 18.8.	Loss of key persons	lkp	F4	Organizational distrust
Q 18.9.	Lack of motivation	m	F2	Future insecurity
Q 18.10.	Poor integration leadership	il	F1	Organizational reliability
Q 18.11.	Low organizational identification	oi	F1	Organizational reliability
Q 18.12.	Low intercultural synergy	is	F3	Resistance barriers
Q 18.13.	Increase in absenteeism	a	F3	Resistance barriers
Q 18.14.	Resistance to change	rc	F3	Resistance barriers
Q 18.15.	Sabotage	s	F3	Resistance barriers

The unrotated factor loadings show high positive and high negative loadings on the first two factors (Figure 6).

The four rotated factors are just as good as the initial factors in explaining and reproducing the observed correlation matrix. In the rotated factors table, Coordination/integration, Integration leadership, Professional trust, Communication and Organizational identification (Q 18.3, Q 18.10, Q 18.4, Q 18.7 and Q 18.11) all have high positive loadings on the first factor, Uncertainty about the future, Goals and objectives and Motivation (Q 18.1, Q 18.2 and Q 18.9) all have high positive loadings on the second factor, Absenteeism, Sabotage, Intercultural synergy and Resistance to change (Q

18.13, Q 18.15, Q 18.12 and Q 18.14) all have high positive loadings on the third factor, Mistrust in advancement opportunities, Mistrust in rewards system, Loss of key persons (Q 18.6, Q 18.5 and Q 18.8) all have high positive loadings on the fourth factor.

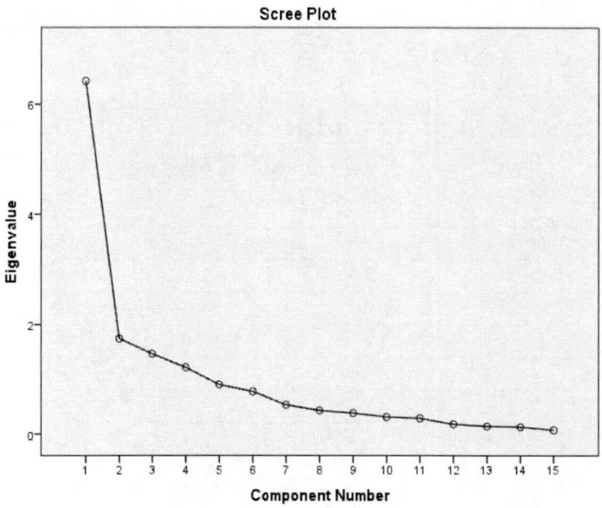

Figure 6. Scree plot for Organizational problems in own company as result of the merger/acquisition.

It can be recognized the first rotated factor (F1) as "Organizational reliability", the second rotated factor (F2) as "Future insecurity", the third rotated factor (F3) as "Resistance barriers" the fourth rotated factor (F4) as "Organizational distrust."

There are four factor equations (Table no. 19):

$$\mathbf{F1} = -0.056 * \mathbf{uaf} - 0.039 * \mathbf{go} + 0.285 * \mathbf{ci} + 0.277 * \mathbf{pt} + 0.095 * \mathbf{mrs} - 0.071 * \mathbf{mao} + 0.176 * \mathbf{c} - 0.162 * \mathbf{lkp} - 0.007 * \mathbf{m} + 0.248 * \mathbf{il} + 0.179 * \mathbf{oi} + 0.103 * \mathbf{is} - 0.044 * \mathbf{a} - 0.041 * \mathbf{rc} - 0.187 * \mathbf{s} \qquad (10)$$

$$\mathbf{F2} = 0.434 * \mathbf{uaf} + 0.405 * \mathbf{go} - 0.087 * \mathbf{ci} - 0.012 * \mathbf{pt} - 0.123 * \mathbf{mrs} - 0.137 * \mathbf{mao} - 0.107 * \mathbf{c} + 0.277 * \mathbf{lkp} + 0.180 * \mathbf{m} - 0.072 * \mathbf{il} + 0.133 * \mathbf{oi} - 0.018 * \mathbf{is} - 0.172 * \mathbf{a} - 0.041 * \mathbf{rc} + 0.135 * \mathbf{s} \qquad (11)$$

F3 = -0.039 * **uaf** - 0.019 * **go** - 0.036 * **ci** - 0.224 * **pt** - 0.083 * **mrs** + 0.053 * **mao** + 0.042* **c** -0.155 * **lkp** + 0.030 * **m** + 0.001 * **il** - 0.009 * **oi** + 0.333 * **is** + 0.419 * **a** + 0.262 * rc + 0.354 * **s** (12)

F4 = -0.117 * **uaf** - 0.143 * **go** - 0.068 * **ci** + 0.034 * **pt** + 0.378* **mrs** + 0.486 * **mao** + 0.086* **c** + 0.357* **lkp** + 0.082 * **m** - 0.039 * **il** - 0.177 * **oi** - 0.306 * **is** + 0.079 * **a** + 0.015 * rc - 0.057 * **s** (13)

Table 19. Component Score Coefficient Matrix for Organizational problems in own company as result of the merger/acquisition

	Component			
	1	**2**	**3**	**4**
Q 18.1	-.056	.434	-.039	-.117
Q 18.2	-.039	.405	-.019	-.143
Q 18.3	.285	-.087	-.036	-.068
Q 18.4	.277	-.012	-.224	.034
Q 18.5	.095	-.123	-.083	.378
Q 18.6	-.071	-.137	.053	.486
Q 18.7	.176	-.107	.042	.086
Q 18.8	-.162	.277	-.155	.357
Q 18.9	-.007	.180	.030	.082
Q 18.10	.248	-.072	.001	-.039
Q 18.11	.179	.133	-.009	-.177
Q 18.12	.103	-.018	.333	-.306
Q 18.13	-.044	-.172	.419	.079
Q 18.14	-.041	-.041	.262	.015
Q 18.15	-.187	.135	.354	-.057

6.7. THE ORGANIZATIONAL PROBLEMS IN THE OTHER COMPANY AS RESULT OF THE MERGER/ACQUISITION DIMENSION

The factors come from the questionnaire item below:

As a result of the merger/acquisition, have there been following organizational problems in the other company?

Table 20. Factors and corresponding items for Organizational problems in the other company as result of the merger/acquisition

Item number	Item name	Item code	Factor	Factor name
Q 19.1.	Uncertainty about the future	uaf	F3	Future insecurity
Q 19.2.	Divergent goals and objectives	go	F3	Future insecurity
Q 19.3.	Poor coordination/integration	ci	F1	Organizational reliability
Q 19.4.	Low professional trust	pt	F1	Organizational reliability
Q 19.5.	Mistrust in rewards system	mrs	F2	Organizational distrust
Q 19.6.	Mistrust in advancement opportunities	mao	F2	Organizational distrust
Q 19.7.	Poor communication	c	F1	Organizational reliability
Q 19.8.	Loss of key persons	lkp	F2	Organizational distrust
Q 19.9.	Lack of motivation	m	F3	Future insecurity
Q 19.10.	Poor integration leadership	il	F1	Organizational reliability
Q 19.11.	Low organizational identification	oi	F1	Organizational reliability
Q 19.12.	Low intercultural synergy	is	F4	Resistance barriers
Q 19.13.	Increase in absenteeism	a	F4	Resistance barriers
Q 19.14.	Resistance to change	rc	F4	Resistance barriers
Q 19.15.	Sabotage	s	F4	Resistance barriers

Table 20 presents the factors and corresponding items for Organizational problems in the other company as result of the merger/acquisition.

In the KMO and Bartlett's Test results for Organizational problems in the other company as result of the merger/acquisition table the value for the "Measure of Sampling Adequacy" is 0.771, and "Bartlett's Test of Sphericity" has an associated P value (Sig. in the table) less than 0.001. A valid factor analysis can be performed.

From the Total Variance Explained results for Organizational problems in the other company as result of the merger/acquisition table four components were extracted. The first four components have eigenvalues over 1.00, that explain more than 70% of the total variability in the data. Four factors formula is correct. The first two factors of the initial solution are much more important than the third and the fourth. The eigenvalues of the rotated factor are 3.524, 3.165, 2.018 and 1.894, compared to 6.165, 1.881, 1.388 and 1.167 in the initial solution.

The unrotated factor loadings show high positive and high negative loadings on the first two factors (Figure 7).

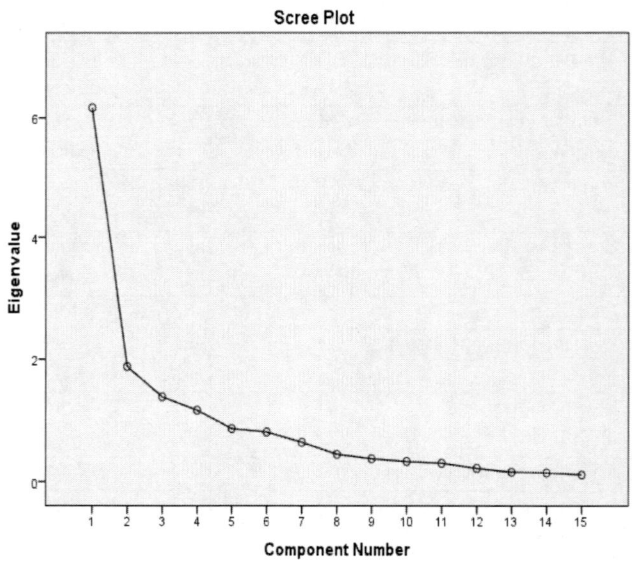

Figure 7. Scree plot for Organizational problems in the other company as result of the merger/acquisition.

The four rotated factors are just as good as the initial factors in explaining and reproducing the observed correlation matrix. In the rotated factors table, Communication, Coordination/integration, Integration leadership, Professional trust and Organizational identification (Q 19.7, Q 19.3, Q 19.10, Q 19.4 and Q 19.11) all have high positive loadings on the first factor, Mistrust in advancement opportunities, Mistrust in rewards system, Loss of key persons (Q 19.6, Q 19.5 and Q 19.8) all have high positive loadings on the second factor, Goals and objectives, Uncertainty about the future and Motivation (Q 19.2, Q 19.1 and Q 19.9) all have high positive loadings on the third factor, Sabotage, Absenteeism, Resistance to change and Intercultural synergy (Q 19.15, Q 19.13, Q 19.14 and Q 19.12) all have high positive loadings on the fourth factor.

It can be recognized the first rotated factor (F1) as "Organizational reliability", the second rotated factor (F2) as "Organizational distrust", the third rotated factor (F3) as "Future insecurity", the fourth rotated factor (F4) as "Resistance barriers".

Table 21. Component Score Coefficient Matrix for Organizational problems in the other company as result of the merger/acquisition

Component Score Coefficient Matrix				
	Component			
	1	**2**	**3**	**4**
Q 19.1	-.132	.004	.479	-.058
Q 19.2	-.024	-.087	.458	.028
Q 19.3	.255	-.134	.147	-.035
Q 19.4	.188	-.179	.258	-.052
Q 19.5	-.102	.223	-.131	.218
Q 19.6	-.041	.341	-.021	-.165
Q 19.7	.302	-.043	-.083	-.077
Q 19.8	-.057	.146	.114	.026
Q 19.9	.014	.268	-.005	-.119
Q 19.10	.247	-.022	-.092	.047
Q 19.11	-.062	.353	-.094	-.065
Q 19.12	.211	.158	-.284	-.074
Q 19.13	-.111	-.013	-.014	.516
Q 19.14	.226	-.016	-.056	-.044
Q 19.15	-.012	-.187	.001	.566

There are four factor equations (Table 21):

F1 = -0.132 * **uaf** - 0.024 * **go** + 0.255 * **ci** + 0.188 * **pt** - 0.102* **mrs** - 0.041 * **mao** + 0.302* **c** -0.057* **lkp** + 0.014 * **m** + 0.247 * **il** - 0.062 * **oi** + 0.211 * **is** - 0.111 * **a** + 0.226 * **rc** - 0.012 * **s** (14)

F2 = 0.004 * **uaf** - 0.087 * **go** - 0.134 * **ci** - 0.179 * **pt** + 0.223* **mrs** + 0.341 * **mao** - 0.043 * **c** + 0.146* **lkp** + 0.268 * **m** - 0.022 * **il** + 0.353 * **oi** + 0.158 * **is** - 0.013 * **a** - 0.016 * **rc** - 0.187 * **s** (15)

F3 = 0.479 * **uaf** + 0.458 * **go** + 0.147 * **ci** + 0.258 * **pt** - 0.131 * **mrs** - 0.021 * **mao** - 0.083* **c** + 0.114 * **lkp** - 0.005 * **m** - 0.092 * **il** - 0.094 * **oi** - 0.284 * **is** - 0.014 * **a** - 0.056 * **rc** + 0.001 * **s** (16)

F4 = -0.058 * **uaf** + 0.028 * **go** - 0.035 * **ci** - 0.052 * **pt** + 0.218* **mrs** - 0.165 * **mao** - 0.077* **c** + 0.026* **lkp** - 0.119 * **m** + 0.047 * **il** - 0.065 * **oi** - 0.074 * **is** + 0.516 * **a** - 0.044 * **rc** + 0.566 * **s** (17)

6.8. The Problems in Cooperation between the Two Teams of Top Managers Dimension

The factors come from the questionnaire item below:

In your opinion, have there been problems in cooperation between the two teams of top managers?

Table 22 presents the factors and corresponding items for Problems in cooperation between the two teams of top managers.

Table 22. Factors and corresponding items for Problems in cooperation between the two teams of top managers

Item number	Item name	Item code	Factor	Factor name
Q 20.1.	Misunderstandings	mu	F1	Conflict prevention
Q 20.2.	Mistrust	mt	F1	Conflict prevention
Q 20.3.	Incapacity to reconcile different points of view	irpw	F1	Conflict prevention
Q 20.4.	Unwillingness to reconcile different points of view	urpw	F1	Conflict prevention
Q 20.5.	Conflicts	c	F1	Conflict prevention

In the KMO and Bartlett's Test results for Problems in cooperation between the two teams of top managers table the value for the "Measure of Sampling Adequacy" is 0.801, and "Bartlett's Test of Sphericity" has an associated P value (Sig. in the table) less than 0.001. A valid factor analysis can be performed.

From the Total Variance Explained results for Problems in cooperation between the two teams of top managers table one component was extracted. The first component has eigenvalue over 1.00, that explain more than 63% of the total variability in the data. One factor formula is correct.

The unrotated factor loadings show high positive loadings on the first factor (Figure 8).

Unwillingness to reconcile different points of view, Incapacity to reconcile different points of view, Mistrust, Conflicts and Misunderstandings (Q 20.4, Q 20.3, Q 20.2, Q 20.5 and Q 20.1) all have high positive loadings on the factor.

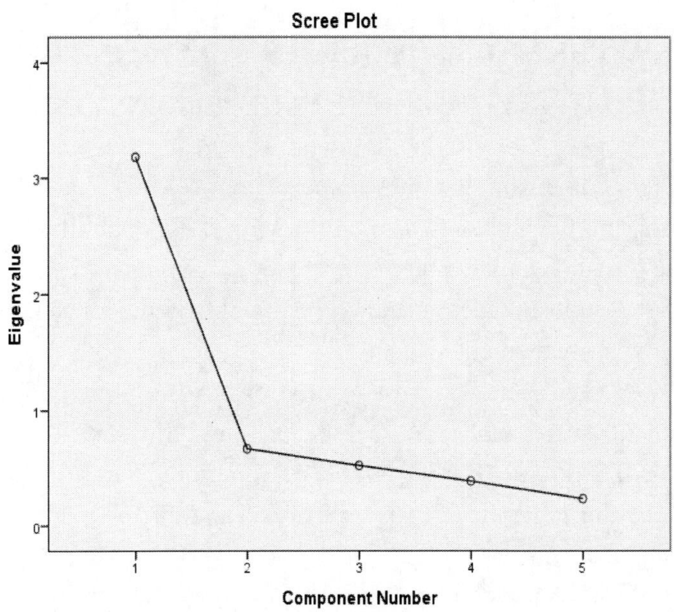

Figure 8. Scree plot for Problems in cooperation between the two teams of top managers.

It can be recognized the factor (F1) as "Conflict prevention".

There is a factor equation (Table 23):

$$\mathbf{F1} = 0.236 * \mathbf{mu} + 0.252 * \mathbf{mt} + 0.253 * \mathbf{irpw} + 0.270 * \mathbf{urpw} + 0.242 * \mathbf{c} \quad (18)$$

Table 23. Component Score Coefficient Matrix for Problems in cooperation between the two teams of top managers

	Component
	1
Q 20.1	.236
Q 20.2	.252
Q 20.3	.253
Q 20.4	.270
Q 20.5	.242

6.9. The Skills/Abilities Useful in the Post-Investment Stage Dimension

The factors come from the questionnaire item below:

In your opinion, which ones of the following skills or abilities have been useful in the post-investment stage?

Table 24 presents the factors and corresponding items for Skills/abilities useful in the post-investment stage.

In the KMO and Bartlett's Test results for Skills/abilities useful in the post-investment stage table the value for the "Measure of Sampling Adequacy" is 0.874, and "Bartlett's Test of Sphericity" has an associated P value (Sig. in the table) less than 0.001. A valid factor analysis can be performed.

From the Total Variance Explained results for Skills/abilities useful in the post-investment stage table One component was extracted. The first component has eigenvalue over 1.00, that explain more than 60% of the total variability in the data. One factor formula is correct.

Table 24. Factors and corresponding items for Skills/abilities useful in the post-investment stage

Item number	Item name	Item code	Factor	Factor name
Q 16.1.	Cultural differences understanding	cdu	F1	Intercultural competence
Q 16.2.	Multilingualism	m	F1	Intercultural competence
Q 16.3.	Adaptation to a different culture	adc	F1	Intercultural competence
Q 16.4.	Awareness of own culture	aoc	F1	Intercultural competence
Q 16.5.	Respect for otherness	ro	F1	Intercultural competence
Q 16.6.	Communicative awareness	ca	F1	Intercultural competence
Q 16.7.	Behavioral flexibility	bf	F1	Intercultural competence
Q 16.8.	Readiness for change	rc	F1	Intercultural competence

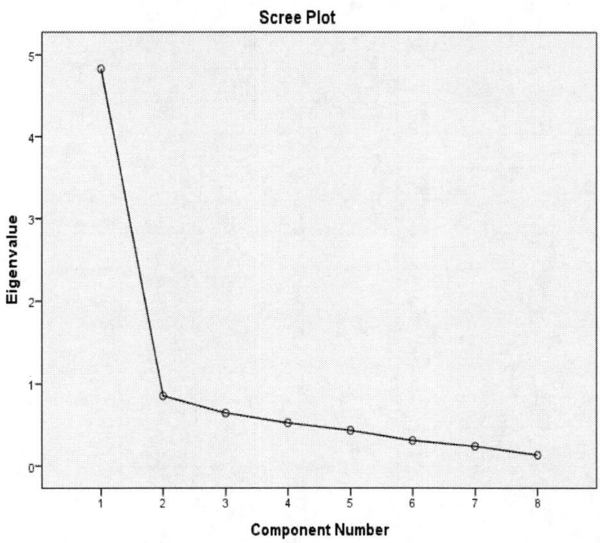

Figure 9. Scree plot for Skills/abilities useful in the post-investment stage.

The unrotated factor loadings show high positive loadings on the first factor (Figure 9).

Readiness for change, Respect for otherness, Adaptation to a different culture, Communicative awareness, Cultural differences understanding, Awareness of own culture, Behavioral flexibility, Multilingualism (Q 16.8, Q 16.5, Q 16.3, Q 16.6 , Q 16.1, Q 16.4 , Q 16.7 and Q 16.2) all have high positive loadings on the factor.

It can be recognized the factor (F1) as "Intercultural competence."

There is a factor equation (Table 25):

$$\mathbf{F1} = 0.157 * \mathbf{cdu} + 0.110 * \mathbf{m} + 0.175 * \mathbf{adc} + 0.154 * \mathbf{aoc} + 0.177 * \mathbf{ro} + 0.175 * \mathbf{ca} + 0.151 * \mathbf{bf} + 0.178 * \mathbf{rc} \quad (19)$$

Table 25. Component Score Coefficient Matrix for Skills/abilities useful in the post-investment stage

	Component
	1
Q 16.1	.157
Q 16.2	.110
Q 16.3	.175
Q 16.4	.154
Q 16.5	.177
Q 16.6	.175
Q 16.7	.151
Q 16.8	.178

Chapter 7

CULTURAL DIFFERENCES AND SYNERGY EFFECTS

7.1. ORGANIZATIONAL FUNCTIONS AND CORE VALUES IN THE POST-INVESTMENT STAGE DEPENDENCE OF ORGANIZATIONAL FUNCTIONS AND CORE VALUES BEFORE THE MERGER/ACQUISITION

The Model Summary for Organizational functions and core values in the post-investment stage by Organizational functions and core values before the merger/acquisition table provides an overview of the results. Of primary interest are the R Square and Adjusted R Square values. The Correlation (R = .234), the Correlation squared (R^2 = .055), the adjusted Correlation squared (adj.R^2 = .032), and the Standard Error of the Estimate can be used to determine how well a regression model fits the data. The correlation coefficient R can be considered to be one measure of the quality of the prediction of the dependent variable. A value of 0.234 indicates a low level of prediction. The R2 value (also called the coefficient of determination) is the proportion of variance in the dependent variable that can be explained by the independent variable (technically, it is the proportion of variation accounted for by the regression model above and beyond the mean model).

The value of 0.055 indicates that the independent variable explains 5.5% of the variability of the dependent variable.

The ANOVA for Organizational functions and core values in the post-investment stage by Organizational functions and core values before the merger/acquisition table indicates that the regression model predicts the dependent variable significantly well. The p value indicates the statistical significance of the regression model that was run. Here, p = 0.130 indicates that, overall, the regression model statistically significantly predicts the outcome variable. It is a good fit for the data.

Table 26. Coefficients for Organizational functions and core values in the post-investment stage by Organizational functions and core values before the merger/acquisition

Model		Unstandardized Coefficients		Standardized Coefficients	t	Sig.
		B	Std. Error	Beta		
1	(Constant)	-.009	.150		-.060	.952
	Organizational functions and core values before the merger/acquisition	.243	.157	.234	1.544	.130

Table 26 presents the Coefficients for Organizational functions and core values in the post-investment stage by Organizational functions and core values before the merger/acquisition. It provides with the necessary information to predict Organizational functions and core values in the post-investment stage from Organizational functions and core values before the merger/acquisition, as well as determine whether Organizational functions and core values before the merger/acquisition contributes statistically significantly to the model (by looking at the "Sig."column). Furthermore, we can use the values in the "B" column under the "Unstandardized Coefficients" column to present the regression equation as:

(Organizational functions and core values in the post-investment stage) = 0.243 *

(Organizational functions and core values before the merger/acquisition) - 0.009 (20)

Figure 10 presents the Normal P-P Plot of Regression Standardized Residual values for Organizational functions and core values in the post-investment stage by Organizational functions and core values before the merger/acquisition. It shows that the values are very close to the reference line, which indicates very little deviation of the expected values from the observed values.

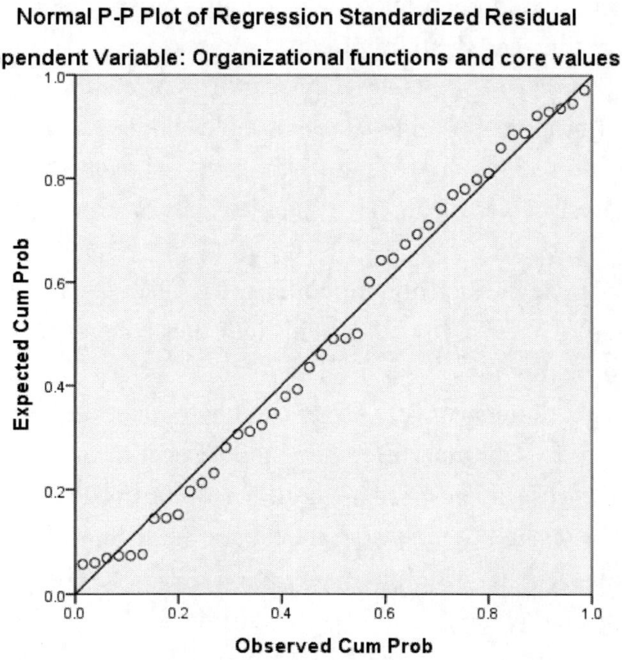

Figure 10. Normal P-P Plot of Regression Standardized Residual values for Organizational functions and core values in the post-investment stage by Organizational functions and core values before the merger/acquisition.

7.2. Organizational Functions in the Post-Investment Stage Dependence of Cultural Differences and Respect in Own Company and Cultural Differences and Respect in the Other Company

In the Correlations for Organizational functions in the post-investment stage by Cultural differences and respect in own company and Cultural differences and respect in the other company table the correlation results are divided into three major rows: the first contains the Pearson r values, the second contains the probabilities of obtaining those values if the null hypothesis was true, and the third provides sample size.

The correlation matrix table includes the correlation, p-value, and number of observations for each pair of variables in the model. For unequal number of observations for each pair, SPSS removes cases from the regression analysis which do not have complete data on all variables selected for the model.

It can be noticed the lack of multicollinearity. The two predictors are not strongly related ($r = -.176$, $p = .142$). This indicates adherence to one of the assumptions of regression.

The Model Summary for Organizational functions in the post-investment stage by Cultural differences and respect in own company and Cultural differences and respect in the other company table provides an overview of the results. Of primary interest are the R Square and Adjusted R Square values. The Multiple Correlation ($R = .065$), the Multiple Correlation squared ($R^2 = .004$), the adjusted Multiple Correlation squared (adj.$R^2 = -.051$), and the Standard Error of the Estimate can be used to determine how well a regression model fits the data. The multiple correlation coefficient R can be considered to be one measure of the quality of the prediction of the dependent variable. A value of 0.065 indicates a low level of prediction.

The R2 value (also called the coefficient of determination) is the proportion of variance in the dependent variable that can be explained by the independent variables (technically, it is the proportion of variation accounted for by the regression model above and beyond the mean model). The value of 0.004 indicates that the independent variables explain 0.4% of the variability of the dependent variable.

The multiple correlation refers to the combined correlation of each predictor with the outcome. The multiple correlation squared represents the amount of variance in the outcome which is accounted for by the predictors; here, 0.4% of the variance in Organizational functions in the post-investment stage is accounted for by both Cultural differences and respect in own company and Cultural differences and respect in the other company. However, the multiple correlation squared is a bit optimistic, and therefore, the adjusted R^2 is more appropriate.

The ANOVA for Organizational functions in the post-investment stage by Cultural differences and respect in own company and Cultural differences and respect in the other company table shows the test of significance of the model using an ANOVA. There are 38 (N - 1) total degrees of freedom. With two predictors, the Regression effect has two degrees of freedom. The Regression effect is statistically significant indicating that prediction of the dependent variable is accomplished better than can be done by chance.

The *F*-ratio in the **ANOVA** table tests whether the overall regression model is a good fit for the data. The table shows that the independent variables statistically significantly do not predict the dependent variable, F (2, 36) = .076, p = *0.927* (the regression model is not a good fit of the data).

Table 27 presents the Coefficients for Organizational functions in the post-investment stage by Cultural differences and respect in own company and Cultural differences and respect in the other company. The first two columns contain unstandardized (or raw score) coefficients and their standard errors. Unstandardized coefficients indicate how much the dependent variable varies with an independent variable when all other independent variables are held constant. The Constant coefficient is simply the y-intercept term for a linear best fit fine representing our fitted model. The Cultural differences and respect in own company and Cultural differences and respect in the other company unstandardized coefficients represent the weight applied to each score (for each variable) to produce new Organizational functions in the post-investment stage scores along the best fit line. The unstandardized coefficients are used to build the linear regression equation one might use to predict new scores of Organizational functions in the post-investment stage using available scores of Cultural differences and respect in own company and Cultural differences and respect in the other company. The equation is below:

(Organizational functions in the post-investment stage) = .067 *
(Cultural differences and respect in own company) + .013 *
(Cultural differences and respect in the other company) + .034 (21)

Table 27. Coefficients for Organizational functions in the post-investment stage by Cultural differences and respect in own company and Cultural differences and respect in the other company

Model		Unstandardized Coefficients		Standardized Coefficients	t	Sig.
		B	Std. Error	Beta		
1	(Constant)	.034	.168		.200	.843
	Cultural differences and respect in own company	.067	.171	.066	.389	.699
	Cultural differences and respect in the other company	.013	.178	.012	.073	.942

The Standardized Coefficients, which are typically reported in social science journals (rather than the unstandardized coefficients) as a way of interpreting variable importance because, they can be directly compared (they are in the same metric). The standardized coefficients use the symbol Beta, which is the capital Greek letter β and can be interpreted as the correlation between a predictor and the outcome variable. There is no constant or y-intercept term when referring to standardized scores because, the y-intercept when graphing them is always zero. The standardization transformation results in a mean of 0 and a standard deviation of 1 for all variables so transformed.

The *Y* intercept of the raw score model is labelled as the Constant and has a value of .034. Of primary interest here are the raw (B) and standardized (Beta) coefficients, and their significance levels determined by *t* tests. The predictors are not statistically significant.

The calculated t-score for each unstandardized coefficient (coefficient divided by standard error) and their associated p-value are presented in the last two columns.

Figure 11 presents the Normal P-P Plot of Regression Standardized Residual values for Organizational functions in the post-investment stage by Cultural differences and respect in own company and Cultural differences and respect in the other company. It shows that the values are very close to the reference line, which indicates very little deviation of the expected values from the observed values.

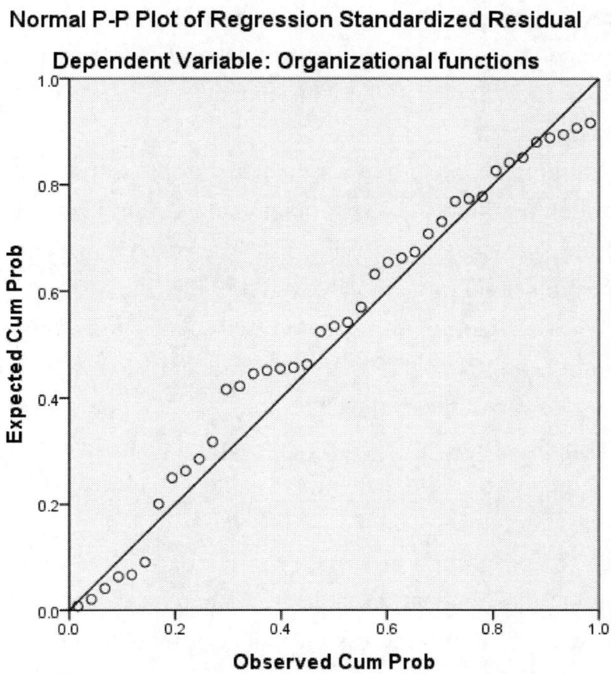

Figure 11. Normal P-P Plot of Regression Standardized Residual values for Organizational functions in the post-investment stage by Cultural differences and respect in own company and Cultural differences and respect in the other company.

7.3. Organizational Functions in the Post-Investment Stage Dependence of Group Identification in Own Company and Group Identification in the Other Company

In the Correlations for Organizational functions in the post-investment stage by Group identification in own company and Group identification in the other company table the correlation results are divided into three major rows: the first contains the Pearson r values, the second contains the probabilities of obtaining those values if the null hypothesis was true, and the third provides sample size.

The correlation matrix table includes the correlation, p-value, and number of observations for each pair of variables in the model. For unequal number of observations for each pair, SPSS removes cases from the regression analysis which do not have complete data on all variables selected for the model.

It can be noticed the lack of multicollinearity. The two predictors are not strongly related ($r = .178, p = .139$). This indicates adherence to one of the assumptions of regression.

The Model Summary for Organizational functions in the post-investment stage by Group identification in own company and Group identification in the other company table provides an overview of the results. Of primary interest are the R Square and Adjusted R Square values. It provides the Multiple Correlation ($R = .410$), the Multiple Correlation squared ($R^2 = .168$), the adjusted Multiple Correlation squared (adj.$R^2 = .122$), and the Standard Error of the Estimate which can be used to determine how well a regression model fits the data. The multiple correlation coefficient R can be considered to be one measure of the quality of the prediction of the dependent variable. A value of .410 indicates a medium level of prediction. The R2 value (also called the coefficient of determination) is the proportion of variance in the dependent variable that can be explained by the independent variables (technically, it is the proportion of variation accounted for by the regression model above and beyond the mean model). The value of 0.168 indicates that the independent variables explain 16.8% of the variability of the dependent variable.

The multiple correlation refers to the combined correlation of each predictor with the outcome. The multiple correlation squared represents the amount of variance in the outcome which is accounted for by the predictors; here, 16.8% of the variance in Organizational functions in the post-investment stage is accounted for by both Group identification in own company and Group identification in the other company. However, the multiple correlation squared is a bit optimistic, and therefore, the adjusted R^2 is more appropriate.

The ANOVA for Organizational functions in the post-investment stage by Group identification in own company and Group identification in the other company table shows the test of significance of the model using an ANOVA. There are 38 (N - 1) total degrees of freedom. With two predictors, the Regression effect has two degrees of freedom. The Regression effect is statistically significant indicating that prediction of the dependent variable is accomplished better than can be done by chance.

The F-ratio in the **ANOVA** table tests whether the overall regression model is a good fit for the data. The table shows that the independent variables statistically significantly predict the dependent variable, F (2, 36) = 3.633, p = 0.037 (the regression model is a good fit of the data)

Table 28 presents the Coefficients for Organizational functions in the post-investment stage by Group identification in own company and Group identification in the other company. The first two columns contain unstandardized (or raw score) coefficients and their standard errors. Unstandardized coefficients indicate how much the dependent variable varies with an independent variable when all other independent variables are held constant. The Constant coefficient is simply the y-intercept term for a linear best fit fine representing our fitted model. The Group identification in own company and Group identification in the other company unstandardized coefficients represent the weight applied to each score (for each variable) to produce new Organizational functions in the post-investment stage scores along the best fit line. The unstandardized coefficients are used to build the linear regression equation one might use to predict new scores of Organizational functions in the post-investment stage using available scores of Group identification in own company and Group identification in the other company. The equation is below:

$$\text{(Organizational functions in the post-investment stage)} = .433^* \\ \text{(Group identification in own company)} + .061^* \\ \text{(Group identification in the other company)} + .002 \qquad (22)$$

Table 28. Coefficients for Organizational functions in the post-investment stage by Group identification in own company and Group identification in the other company

Model		Unstandardized Coefficients		Standardized Coefficients	t	Sig.
		B	Std. Error	Beta		
1	(Constant)	.002	.154		.011	.991
	Group identification in own company	.433	.170	.394	2.552	.015
	Group identification in the other company	.061	.153	.062	.399	.692

The Standardized Coefficients, which are typically reported in social science journals (rather than the unstandardized coefficients) as a way of interpreting variable importance because, they can be directly compared (they are in the same metric). The standardized coefficients use the symbol Beta, which is the capital Greek letter β and can be interpreted as the correlation between a predictor and the outcome variable. There is no constant or y-intercept term when referring to standardized scores because, the y-intercept when graphing them is always zero. The standardization transformation results in a mean of 0 and a standard deviation of 1 for all variables so transformed.

The *Y* intercept of the raw score model is labelled as the Constant and has a value of .002. Of primary interest here are the raw (B) and standardized (Beta) coefficients, and their significance levels determined by *t* tests. The predictors are not statistically significant except for Group identification in own company.

The calculated t-score for each unstandardized coefficient (coefficient divided by standard error) and their associated p-value are presented in the last two columns.

Figure 12 presents the Normal P-P Plot of Regression Standardized Residual values for Organizational functions in the post-investment stage by Group identification in own company and Group identification in the other company. It shows that the values are very close to the reference line, which indicates very little deviation of the expected values from the observed values.

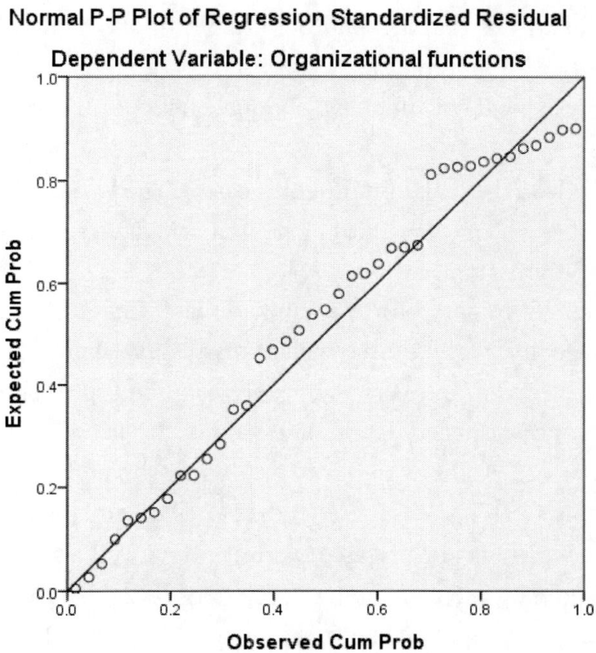

Figure 12. Normal P-P Plot of Regression Standardized Residual values for Organizational functions in the post-investment stage by Group identification in own company and Group identification in the other company.

7.4. Organizational Functions in the Post-Investment Stage Dependence of Agility in Own Company and Agility in the Other Company

In the Correlations for Organizational functions in the post-investment stage by Agility in own company and Agility in the other company table the correlation results are divided into three major rows: the first contains the

Pearson r values, the second contains the probabilities of obtaining those values if the null hypothesis was true, and the third provides sample size.

The correlation matrix table includes the correlation, p-value, and number of observations for each pair of variables in the model. For unequal number of observations for each pair, SPSS removes cases from the regression analysis which do not have complete data on all variables selected for the model.

It can be noticed the lack of multicollinearity. The two predictors are not strongly related ($r = .075$, $p = .326$). This indicates adherence to one of the assumptions of regression.

The Model Summary for Organizational functions in the post-investment stage by Agility in own company and Agility in the other company table provides an overview of the results. Of primary interest are the R Square and Adjusted R Square values. It provides the Multiple Correlation ($R = .233$), the Multiple Correlation squared ($R^2 = .054$), the adjusted Multiple Correlation squared (adj.R^2 =.002), and the Standard Error of the Estimate which can be used to determine how well a regression model fits the data. The multiple correlation coefficient R can be considered to be one measure of the quality of the prediction of the dependent variable. A value of .233 indicates a medium level of prediction.

The R2 value (also called the coefficient of determination) is the proportion of variance in the dependent variable that can be explained by the independent variables (technically, it is the proportion of variation accounted for by the regression model above and beyond the mean model). The value of 0.054 indicates that the independent variables explain 5.4% of the variability of the dependent variable.

The multiple correlation refers to the combined correlation of each predictor with the outcome. The multiple correlation squared represents the amount of variance in the outcome which is accounted for by the predictors; here, 5.4% of the variance in Organizational functions in the post-investment stage is accounted for by both Agility in own company and Agility in the other company. However, the multiple correlation squared is a bit optimistic, and therefore, the adjusted R^2 is more appropriate.

The ANOVA for Organizational functions in the post-investment stage by Agility in own company and Agility in the other company table shows the test of significance of the model using an ANOVA. There are 38 (N - 1) total degrees of freedom. With two predictors, the Regression effect has two degrees of freedom. The Regression effect is statistically significant indicating that prediction of the dependent variable is accomplished better than can be done by chance. The *F*-ratio in the ANOVA table tests whether the overall regression model is a good fit for the data. The table shows that the independent variables statistically significantly do not predict the dependent variable, $F\,(2, 36) = 1.037$, $p = 0.365$ (the regression model is not a good fit of the data).

Table 29 presents the Coefficients for Organizational functions in the post-investment stage by Agility in own company and Agility in the other company. The first two columns contain unstandardized (or raw score) coefficients and their standard errors. Unstandardized coefficients indicate how much the dependent variable varies with an independent variable when all other independent variables are held constant. The Constant coefficient is simply the y-intercept term for a linear best fit fine representing our fitted model. The Agility in own company and Agility in the other company unstandardized coefficients represent the weight applied to each score (for each variable) to produce new Organizational functions in the post-investment stage scores along the best fit line. The unstandardized coefficients are used to build the linear regression equation one might use to predict new scores of Organizational functions in the post-investment stage using available scores of Agility in own company and Agility in the other company. The equation is below:

$$\begin{aligned}&(\text{Organizational functions in the post-investment stage}) = -.058 \ast \\&(\text{Agility in own company}) + .226 \ast \\&(\text{Agility in the other company}) + .045\end{aligned} \qquad (23)$$

The Standardized Coefficients, which are typically reported in social science journals (rather than the unstandardized coefficients) as a way of interpreting variable importance because, they can be directly compared (they are in the same metric). The standardized coefficients use the symbol Beta, which is the capital Greek letter β and can be interpreted as the correlation between a predictor and the outcome variable. There is no constant or y-intercept term when referring to standardized scores because, the y-intercept when graphing them is always zero. The standardization transformation results in a mean of 0 and a standard deviation of 1 for all variables so transformed.

The *Y* intercept of the raw score model is labelled as the Constant and has a value of .045. Of primary interest here are the raw (B) and standardized (Beta) coefficients, and their significance levels determined by *t* tests. The predictors are not statistically significant, except for Agility in the other company.

The calculated t-score for each unstandardized coefficient (coefficient divided by standard error) and their associated p-value are presented in the last two columns.

Table 29. Coefficients for Organizational functions in the post-investment stage by Agility in own company and Agility in the other company

Model		Unstandardized Coefficients		Standardized Coefficients	t	Sig.
		B	Std. Error	Beta		
1	(Constant)	.045	.164		.272	.787
	Agility in own company	-.058	.167	-.057	-.348	.730
	Agility in the other company	.226	.159	.231	1.420	.164

Figure 13 presents the Normal P-P Plot of Regression Standardized Residual values for Organizational functions in the post-investment stage by Agility in own company and Agility in the other company. It shows that the values are very close to the reference line, which indicates very little deviation of the expected values from the observed values.

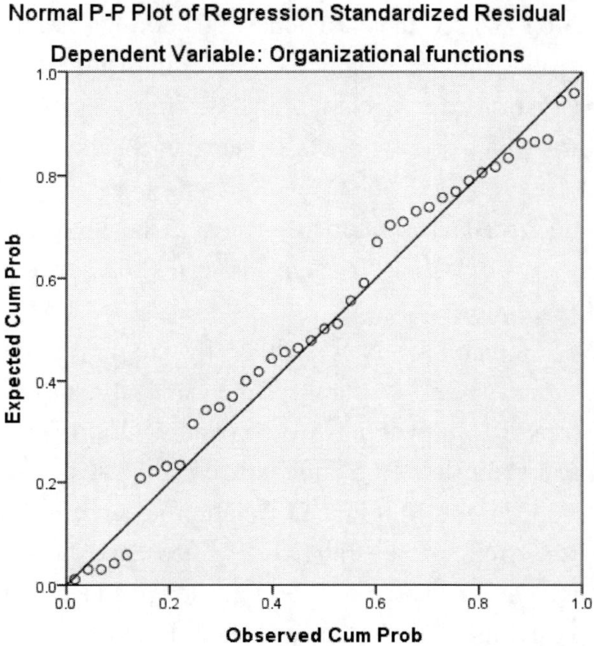

Figure 13. Normal P-P Plot of Regression Standardized Residual values for Organizational functions in the post-investment stage by Agility in own company and Agility in the other company.

7.5. New Culture Dependence of Cultural Differences and Respect in Own Company and Cultural Differences and Respect in the Other Company

In the Correlations for New culture by Cultural differences and respect in own company and Cultural differences and respect in the other company table the correlation results are divided into three major rows: the first contains the Pearson r values, the second contains the probabilities of obtaining those values if the null hypothesis was true, and the third provides sample size.

The correlation matrix table includes the correlation, p-value, and number of observations for each pair of variables in the model. For unequal number of observations for each pair, SPSS removes cases from the regression analysis which do not have complete data on all variables selected for the model.

It can be noticed the lack of multicollinearity. The two predictors are not strongly related ($r = -.193$, $p = .116$). This indicates adherence to one of the assumptions of regression.

The Model Summary for New culture by Cultural differences and respect in own company and Cultural differences and respect in the other company table provides an overview of the results. Of primary interest are the R Square and Adjusted R Square values. It provides the Multiple Correlation ($R = .337$), the Multiple Correlation squared ($R^2 = .113$), the adjusted Multiple Correlation squared (adj.$R^2 =.065$), and the Standard Error of the Estimate which can be used to determine how well a regression model fits the data. The multiple correlation coefficient R can be considered to be one measure of the quality of the prediction of the dependent variable. A value of .337 indicates a medium level of prediction.

The R2 value (also called the coefficient of determination) is the proportion of variance in the dependent variable that can be explained by the independent variables (technically, it is the proportion of variation accounted for by the regression model above and beyond the mean model). The value of 0.113 indicates that the independent variables explain 11.3% of the variability of the dependent variable.

The multiple correlation refers to the combined correlation of each predictor with the outcome. The multiple correlation squared represents the amount of variance in the outcome which is accounted for by the predictors; here, 11.3% of the variance in New culture is accounted for by both Cultural differences and respect in own company and Cultural differences and respect in the other company. However, the multiple correlation squared is a bit optimistic, and therefore, the adjusted R^2 is more appropriate.

The ANOVA for New culture by Cultural differences and respect in own company and Cultural differences and respect in the other company table shows the test of significance of the model using an ANOVA. There are 39

(N - 1) total degrees of freedom. With two predictors, the Regression effect has two degrees of freedom. The Regression effect is statistically significant indicating that prediction of the dependent variable is accomplished better than can be done by chance. The *F*-ratio in the ANOVA table tests whether the overall regression model is a good fit for the data. The table shows that the independent variables statistically significantly predict the dependent variable, $F(2, 37) = 2.366$, $p = 0.108$ (the regression model is a good fit of the data).

Table 30 presents the Coefficients for New culture by Cultural differences and respect in own company and Cultural differences and respect in the other company. The first two columns contain unstandardized (or raw score) coefficients and their standard errors. Unstandardized coefficients indicate how much the dependent variable varies with an independent variable when all other independent variables are held constant. The Constant coefficient is simply the y-intercept term for a linear best fit fine representing our fitted model. The Cultural differences and respect in own company and Cultural differences and respect in the other company unstandardized coefficients represent the weight applied to each score (for each variable) to produce new New culture scores along the best fit line. The unstandardized coefficients are used to build the linear regression equation one might use to predict new scores of New culture using available scores of Cultural differences and respect in own company and Cultural differences and respect in the other company. The equation is below:

$$\begin{aligned}&(\text{New culture}) = -.359 * \\ &(\text{Cultural differences and respect in own company}) + .095 * \\ &(\text{Cultural differences and respect in the other company}) + 3.263\end{aligned} \quad (24)$$

The Standardized Coefficients, which are typically reported in social science journals (rather than the unstandardized coefficients) as a way of interpreting variable importance because, they can be directly compared (they are in the same metric). The standardized coefficients use the symbol Beta, which is the capital Greek letter β and can be interpreted as the correlation between a predictor and the outcome variable. There is no constant or y-intercept term when referring to standardized scores because, the y-intercept when graphing them is always zero. The standardization transformation results in a mean of 0 and a standard deviation of 1 for all variables so transformed.

Table 30. Coefficients for New culture by Cultural differences and respect in own company and Cultural differences and respect in the other company

Model		Unstandardized Coefficients		Standardized Coefficients	t	Sig.
		B	Std. Error	Beta		
1	(Constant)	3.263	.177		18.473	.000
	Cultural differences and respect in own company	-.359	.181	-.312	-1.977	.056
	Cultural differences and respect in the other company	.095	.186	.080	.508	.614

The *Y* intercept of the raw score model is labelled as the Constant and has a value of 3.263. Of primary interest here are the raw (B) and standardized (Beta) coefficients, and their significance levels determined by *t* tests. The predictors are statistically significant, except for Cultural differences and respect in the other company.

The calculated t-score for each unstandardized coefficient (coefficient divided by standard error) and their associated p-value are presented in the last two columns.

Figure 14 presents the Normal P-P Plot of Regression Standardized Residual values for New culture by Cultural differences and respect in own company and Cultural differences and respect in the other company. It shows that the values are very close to the reference line, which indicates very little deviation of the expected values from the observed values.

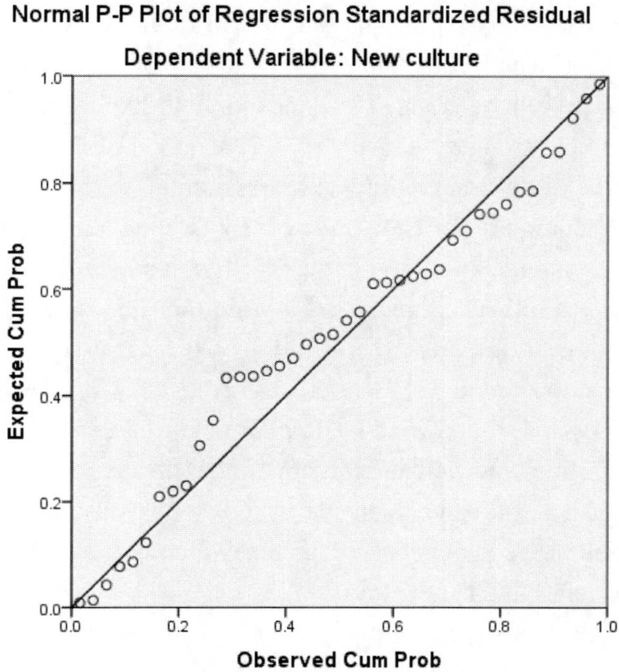

Figure 14. Normal P-P Plot of Regression Standardized Residual values for New culture by Cultural differences and respect in own company and Cultural differences and respect in the other company.

7.6. New Practices Dependence of Group Identification in Own Company and Group Identification in the Other Company

In the Correlations for New practices by Group identification in own company and Group identification in the other company table the correlation results are divided into three major rows: the first contains the Pearson r values, the second contains the probabilities of obtaining those values if the null hypothesis was true, and the third provides sample size.

The correlation matrix table includes the correlation, p-value, and number of observations for each pair of variables in the model. For unequal number of observations for each pair, SPSS removes cases from the regression analysis which do not have complete data on all variables selected for the model. It can be noticed the lack of multicollinearity. The two predictors are not strongly related (r = .171, p = .146). This indicates adherence to one of the assumptions of regression.

The Model Summary for New practices by Group identification in own company and Group identification in the other company table it provides an overview of the results. Of primary interest are the R Square and Adjusted R Square values. It provides the Multiple Correlation (R = .102), the Multiple Correlation squared (R^2 = .010), the adjusted Multiple Correlation squared (adj.R^2 =-.043), and the Standard Error of the Estimate which can be used to determine how well a regression model fits the data. The multiple correlation coefficient R can be considered to be one measure of the quality of the prediction of the dependent variable. A value of .337 indicates a low level of prediction.

The R2 value (also called the coefficient of determination) is the proportion of variance in the dependent variable that can be explained by the independent variables (technically, it is the proportion of variation accounted for by the regression model above and beyond the mean model). The value of .010 indicates that the independent variables explain 1.0% of the variability of the dependent variable.

The multiple correlation refers to the combined correlation of each predictor with the outcome. The multiple correlation squared represents the amount of variance in the outcome which is accounted for by the predictors; here, 1.0% of the variance in New practices is accounted for by both Group identification in own company and Group identification in the other company. However, the multiple correlation squared is a bit optimistic, and therefore, the adjusted R^2 is more appropriate.

The ANOVA for New practices by Group identification in own company and Group identification in the other company table shows the test of significance of the model using an ANOVA. There are 39 (N - 1) total degrees of freedom. With two predictors, the Regression effect has two degrees of freedom. The Regression effect is statistically significant indicating that prediction of the dependent variable is accomplished better than can be done by chance. The *F*-ratio in the ANOVA table tests whether the overall regression model is a good fit for the data. The table shows that the independent variables statistically significantly do not predict the dependent variable, $F(2, 37) = .195$, $p = 0.823$ (the regression model is not a good fit of the data).

Table 31 presents the Coefficients for New practices by Group identification in own company and Group identification in the other company. The first two columns contain unstandardized (or raw score) coefficients and their standard errors. Unstandardized coefficients indicate how much the dependent variable varies with an independent variable when all other independent variables are held constant. The Constant coefficient is simply the y-intercept term for a linear best fit fine representing our fitted model. The Group identification in own company and Group identification in the other company unstandardized coefficients represent the weight applied to each score (for each variable) to produce new New practices scores along the best fit line. The unstandardized coefficients are used to build the linear regression equation one might use to predict new scores of New practices using available scores of Group identification in own company and Group identification in the other company. The equation is below:

(New practices) = .078 *
(Group identification in own company) -.082 *
(Group identification in the other company) + 3.420 (25)

The Standardized Coefficients, which are typically reported in social science journals (rather than the unstandardized coefficients) as a way of interpreting variable importance because, they can be directly compared (they are in the same metric). The standardized coefficients use the symbol Beta, which is the capital Greek letter β and can be interpreted as the correlation between a predictor and the outcome variable. There is no constant or y-intercept term when referring to standardized scores because, the y-intercept when graphing them is always zero. The standardization transformation results in a mean of 0 and a standard deviation of 1 for all variables so transformed.

Table 31. Coefficients for New practices by Group identification in own company and Group identification in the other company

Model		Unstandardized Coefficients		Standardized Coefficients	t	Sig.
		B	Std. Error	Beta		
1	(Constant)	3.420	.159		21.464	.000
	Group identification in own company	.078	.177	.073	.438	.664
	Group identification in the other company	-.082	.159	-.085	-.514	.610

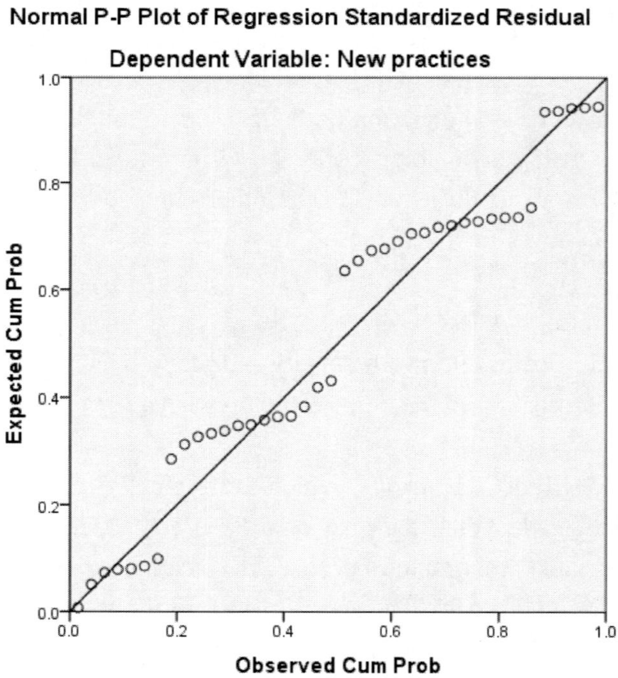

Figure 15. Normal P-P Plot of Regression Standardized Residual values for New practices by Group identification in own company and Group identification in the other company.

The *Y* intercept of the raw score model is labelled as the Constant and has a value of 3.420. Of primary interest here are the raw (B) and standardized (Beta) coefficients, and their significance levels determined by *t* tests. The predictors are not statistically significant, except for Constant. The calculated t-score for each unstandardized coefficient (coefficient divided by standard error) and their associated p-value are presented in the last two columns.

Figure 15 presents the Normal P-P Plot of Regression Standardized Residual values for New practices by Group identification in own company and Group identification in the other company. It shows that the values are very close to the reference line, which indicates very little deviation of the expected values from the observed values.

7.7. Intercultural Synergy Based Decisions Dependence of Cultural Differences and Respect in Own Company and Cultural Differences and Respect in the Other Company

In the Correlations for Intercultural synergy based decisions by Cultural differences and respect in own company and Cultural differences and respect in the other company table the correlation results are divided into three major rows: the first contains the Pearson r values, the second contains the probabilities of obtaining those values if the null hypothesis was true, and the third provides sample size.

The correlation matrix table includes the correlation, p-value, and number of observations for each pair of variables in the model. For unequal number of observations for each pair, SPSS removes cases from the regression analysis which do not have complete data on all variables selected for the model. It can be noticed the lack of multicollinearity. The two predictors are not strongly related (r = -.193, p = .116). This indicates adherence to one of the assumptions of regression.

The Model Summary for Intercultural synergy based decisions by Cultural differences and respect in own company and Cultural differences and respect in the other company table provides an overview of the results. Of primary interest are the R Square and Adjusted R Square values. It provides the Multiple Correlation (R = .155), the Multiple Correlation squared (R^2 = .024), the adjusted Multiple Correlation squared (adj.R^2 =-.029), and the Standard Error of the Estimate which can be used to determine how well a regression model fits the data. The multiple correlation coefficient R can be considered to be one measure of the quality of the prediction of the dependent variable. A value of .155 indicates a low level of prediction.

The R2 value (also called the coefficient of determination) is the proportion of variance in the dependent variable that can be explained by the independent variables (technically, it is the proportion of variation accounted for by the regression model above and beyond the mean model). The value of .024 indicates that the independent variables explain 2.4% of the variability of the dependent variable. The multiple correlation refers to the combined correlation of each predictor with the outcome. The multiple correlation squared represents the amount of variance in the outcome which is accounted for by the predictors; here, 2.4% of the variance in Intercultural synergy based decisions is accounted for by both Cultural differences and respect in own company, Cultural differences and respect in the other company. However, the multiple correlation squared is a bit optimistic, and therefore, the adjusted R^2 is more appropriate.

The ANOVA for Intercultural synergy based decisions by Cultural differences and respect in own company and Cultural differences and respect in the other company table shows the test of significance of the model using an ANOVA. There are 39 (N - 1) total degrees of freedom. With two predictors, the Regression effect has two degrees of freedom. The Regression effect is statistically significant indicating that prediction of the dependent variable is accomplished better than can be done by chance.

The *F*-ratio in the ANOVA table tests whether the overall regression model is a good fit for the data. The table shows that the independent variables statistically significantly do not predict the dependent variable,

F (2, 37) = .457, *p* = 0.637 (the regression model is not a good fit of the data).

Table 32 presents the Coefficients for Intercultural synergy based decisions by Cultural differences and respect in own company and Cultural differences and respect in the other company. The first two columns contain unstandardized (or raw score) coefficients and their standard errors. Unstandardized coefficients indicate how much the dependent variable varies with an independent variable when all other independent variables are held constant. The Constant coefficient is simply the y-intercept term for a linear best fit fine representing our fitted model. The Cultural differences and respect in own company and Cultural differences and respect in the other company unstandardized coefficients represent the weight applied to each score (for each variable) to produce new Intercultural synergy based decisions scores along the best fit line. The unstandardized coefficients are used to build the linear regression equation one might use to predict new scores of Intercultural synergy based decisions using available scores of Cultural differences and respect in own company and Cultural differences and respect in the other company. The equation is below:

(Intercultural synergy based decisions) = -.162 *
(Cultural differences and respect in own company) -.014 *
(Cultural differences and respect in the other company) + 2.897 (26)

Table 32. Coefficients for Intercultural synergy based decisions by Cultural differences and respect in own company and Cultural differences and respect in the other company

Model		Unstandardized Coefficients		Standardized Coefficients	t	Sig.
		B	Std. Error	Beta		
1	(Constant)	2.897	.166		17.473	.000
	Cultural differences and respect in own company	-.162	.170	-.157	-.949	.349
	Cultural differences and respect in the other company	-.014	.175	-.013	-.077	.939

The Standardized Coefficients, which are typically reported in social science journals (rather than the unstandardized coefficients) as a way of interpreting variable importance because, they can be directly compared (they are in the same metric). The standardized coefficients use the symbol Beta, which is the capital Greek letter β and can be interpreted as the correlation between a predictor and the outcome variable. There is no constant or y-intercept term when referring to standardized scores because, the y-intercept when graphing them is always zero. The standardization transformation results in a mean of 0 and a standard deviation of 1 for all variables so transformed.

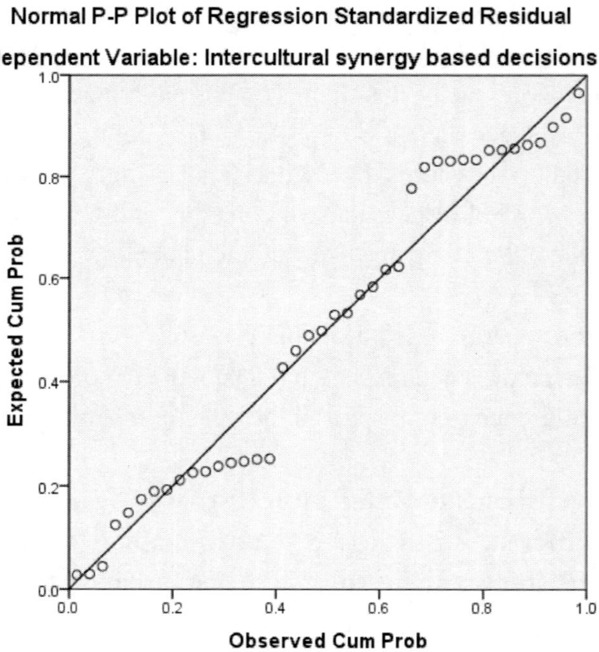

Figure 16. Normal P-P Plot of Regression Standardized Residual values for Intercultural synergy based decisions by Cultural differences and respect in own company and Cultural differences and respect in the other company.

The *Y* intercept of the raw score model is labelled as the Constant and has a value of 2.897. Of primary interest here are the raw (B) and standardized (Beta) coefficients, and their significance levels determined by *t* tests. The predictors are not statistically significant, except for Constant.

The calculated t-score for each unstandardized coefficient (coefficient divided by standard error) and their associated p-value are presented in the last two columns.

Figure 16 presents the Normal P-P Plot of Regression Standardized Residual values for Intercultural synergy based decisions by Cultural differences and respect in own company and Cultural differences and respect in the other company. It shows that the values are very close to the reference line, which indicates very little deviation of the expected values from the observed values.

Chapter 8

CULTURAL DIFFERENCES AND M&A'S OUTCOMES

8.1. ORGANIZATIONAL RELIABILITY IN THE OTHER COMPANY DEPENDENCE OF AGILITY IN OWN COMPANY AND AGILITY IN THE OTHER COMPANY

In the Correlations for Organizational reliability in the other company by Agility in own company and Agility in the other company table the correlation results are divided into three major rows: the first contains the Pearson r values, the second contains the probabilities of obtaining those values if the null hypothesis was true, and the third provides sample size.

The correlation matrix table includes the correlation, p-value, and number of observations for each pair of variables in the model. For unequal number of observations for each pair, SPSS removes cases from the regression analysis which do not have complete data on all variables selected for the model.

It can be noticed the lack of multicollinearity. The two predictors are not strongly related ($r = .070$, $p = .338$). This indicates adherence to one of the assumptions of regression.

The Model Summary for Organizational reliability in the other company by Agility in own company and Agility in the other company table provides an overview of the results. Of primary interest are the R Square and Adjusted R Square values. It provides the Multiple Correlation ($R = .244$), the Multiple Correlation squared ($R^2 = .059$), the adjusted Multiple Correlation squared (adj.$R^2 = .006$), and the Standard Error of the Estimate which can be used to determine how well a regression model fits the data.

The multiple correlation coefficient R can be considered to be one measure of the quality of the prediction of the dependent variable. A value of 0.244 indicates a medium level of prediction. The R2 value (also called the coefficient of determination) is the proportion of variance in the dependent variable that can be explained by the independent variables (technically, it is the proportion of variation accounted for by the regression model above and beyond the mean model). The value of 0.059 indicates that the independent variables explain 5.9% of the variability of the dependent variable.

The multiple correlation refers to the combined correlation of each predictor with the outcome. The multiple correlation squared represents the amount of variance in the outcome which is accounted for by the predictors; here, 5.9% of the variance in Organizational reliability in the other company is accounted for by both Agility in own company and Agility in the other company. However, the multiple correlation squared is a bit optimistic, and therefore, the adjusted R^2 is more appropriate.

The ANOVA for Organizational reliability in the other company by Agility in own company and Agility in the other company table shows the test of significance of the model using an ANOVA. There are 37 (N - 1) total degrees of freedom. With two predictors, the Regression effect has two degrees of freedom. The Regression effect is statistically significant indicating that prediction of the dependent variable is accomplished better than can be done by chance. The *F*-ratio in the ANOVA table tests whether the overall regression model is a good fit for the data. The table shows that the independent variables statistically significantly do not predict the dependent variable, $F\ (2, 35) = 1.104$, $p= 0.343$ (the regression model is not a good fit of the data).

Table 33 presents the Coefficients for Organizational reliability in the other company by Agility in own company and Agility in the other company. The first two columns contain unstandardized (or raw score) coefficients and their standard errors. Unstandardized coefficients indicate how much the dependent variable varies with an independent variable when all other independent variables are held constant. The Constant coefficient is simply the y-intercept term for a linear best fit fine representing our fitted model. The Agility in own company and Agility in the other company unstandardized coefficients represent the weight applied to each score (for each variable) to produce new Organizational reliability in the other company scores along the best fit line. The unstandardized coefficients are used to build the linear regression equation one might use to predict new scores of Organizational reliability in the other company using available scores of Agility in own company and Agility in the other company. The equation is below:

(Organizational reliability in the other company) = .138 *
(Agility in own company) + .190 *
(Agility in the other company) + .057 (27)

Table 33. Coefficients for Organizational reliability in the other company by Agility in own company and Agility in the other company

Model		**Unstandardized Coefficients**		**Standardized Coefficients**	**t**	**Sig.**
		B	**Std. Error**	**Beta**		
1	(Constant)	.057	.168		.337	.738
	Agility in own company	.138	.169	.134	.815	.420
	Agility in the other company	.190	.161	.194	1.182	.245

The Standardized Coefficients, which are typically reported in social science journals (rather than the unstandardized coefficients) as a way of interpreting variable importance because, they can be directly compared (they are in the same metric). The standardized coefficients use the symbol

Beta, which is the capital Greek letter β and can be interpreted as the correlation between a predictor and the outcome variable. There is no constant or y-intercept term when referring to standardized scores because, the y-intercept when graphing them is always zero. The standardization transformation results in a mean of 0 and a standard deviation of 1 for all variables so transformed.

The *Y* intercept of the raw score model is labelled as the Constant and has a value of .057. Of primary interest here are the raw (B) and standardized (Beta) coefficients, and their significance levels determined by *t* tests. The predictors are not statistically significant.

The calculated t-score for each unstandardized coefficient (coefficient divided by standard error) and their associated p-value are presented in the last two columns.

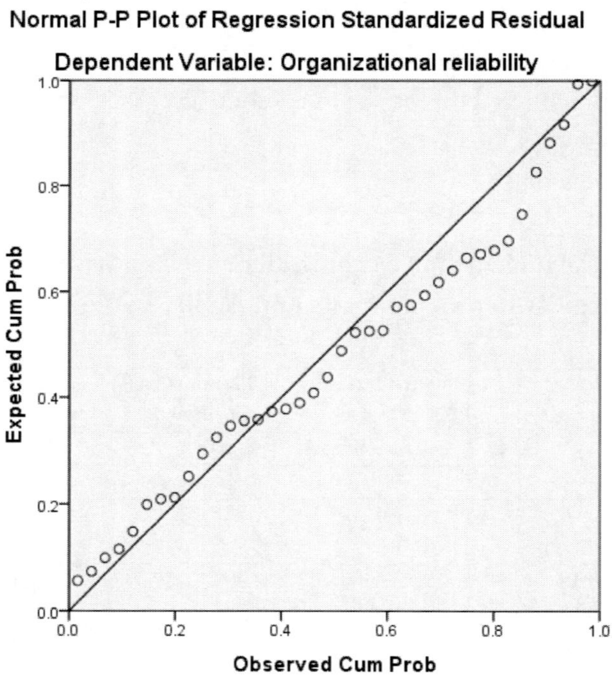

Figure no. 17. Normal P-P Plot of Regression Standardized Residual values for Organizational reliability in the other company by Agility in own company and Agility in the other company.

Figure 17 presents the Normal P-P Plot of Regression Standardized Residual values for Organizational reliability in the other company by Agility in own company and Agility in the other company. It shows that the values are very close to the reference line, which indicates very little deviation of the expected values from the observed values.

8.2. Organizational Reliability in Own Company Dependence of Agility in Own Company and Agility in the Other Company

In the Correlations for Organizational reliability in own company by Agility in own company and Agility in the other company table the correlation results are divided into three major rows: the first contains the Pearson r values, the second contains the probabilities of obtaining those values if the null hypothesis was true, and the third provides sample size.

The correlation matrix table includes the correlation, p-value, and number of observations for each pair of variables in the model. For unequal number of observations for each pair, SPSS removes cases from the regression analysis which do not have complete data on all variables selected for the model. It can be noticed the lack of multicollinearity. The two predictors are not strongly related (r = .053, p= .383). This indicates adherence to one of the assumptions of regression.

The Model Summary for Organizational reliability in own company by Agility in own company and Agility in the other company table provides an overview of the results. Of primary interest are the R Square and Adjusted R Square values. It provides the Multiple Correlation (R = .349), the Multiple Correlation squared (R^2 = .121), the adjusted Multiple Correlation squared (adj.R^2 = .065), and the Standard Error of the Estimate which can be used to determine how well a regression model fits the data.

The multiple correlation coefficient R can be considered to be one measure of the quality of the prediction of the dependent variable. A value of .349 indicates a medium level of prediction. The R2 value (also called the coefficient of determination) is the proportion of variance in the dependent variable that can be explained by the independent variables (technically, it is the proportion of variation accounted for by the regression model above and beyond the mean model). The value of 0.121 indicates that the independent variables explain 12.1% of the variability of the dependent variable.

The multiple correlation refers to the combined correlation of each predictor with the outcome. The multiple correlation squared represents the amount of variance in the outcome which is accounted for by the predictors; here, 12.1% of the variance in Organizational reliability in own company is accounted for by both Agility in own company and Agility in the other company. However, the multiple correlation squared is a bit optimistic, and therefore, the adjusted R^2 is more appropriate.

The ANOVA for Organizational reliability in own company by Agility in own company and Agility in the other company table shows the test of significance of the model using an ANOVA. There are 33 (N - 1) total degrees of freedom. With two predictors, the Regression effect has two degrees of freedom. The Regression effect is statistically significant indicating that prediction of the dependent variable is accomplished better than can be done by chance.

The F-ratio in the ANOVA table tests whether the overall regression model is a good fit for the data. The table shows that the independent variables statistically significantly predict the dependent variable, $F(2, 31) = 2.143$, $p = 0.134$ (the regression model is a good fit of the data).

Table 34 presents the Coefficients for Organizational reliability in own company by Agility in own company and Agility in the other company. The first two columns contain unstandardized (or raw score) coefficients and their standard errors. Unstandardized coefficients indicate how much the dependent variable varies with an independent variable when all other independent variables are held constant. The Constant coefficient is simply the y-intercept term for a linear best fit fine representing our fitted model. The Agility in own company and Agility in the other company unstandardized coefficients represent the weight applied to each score (for each variable) to produce new Organizational reliability in own company scores along the best fit line. The unstandardized coefficients are used to build the linear regression equation one might use to predict new scores of Organizational reliability in own company using available scores of Agility in own company and Agility in the other company. The equation is below:

(Organizational reliability in own company) = .323 *
(Agility in own company) + .087 *
(Agility in the other company) -8.939E-005 (28)

The Standardized Coefficients, which are typically reported in social science journals (rather than the unstandardized coefficients) as a way of interpreting variable importance because, they can be directly compared (they are in the same metric). The standardized coefficients use the symbol Beta, which is the capital Greek letter β and can be interpreted as the correlation between a predictor and the outcome variable. There is no constant or y-intercept term when referring to standardized scores because, the y-intercept when graphing them is always zero. The standardization transformation results in a mean of 0 and a standard deviation of 1 for all variables so transformed.

Table 34. Coefficients for Organizational reliability in own company by Agility in own company and Agility in the other company

Model		Unstandardized Coefficients		Standardized Coefficients	t	Sig.
		B	Std. Error	Beta		
1	(Constant)	-8.939E-005	.166		-.001	1.000
	Agility in own company	.323	.164	.333	1.975	.057
	Agility in the other company	.087	.168	.087	.515	.610

The *Y* intercept of the raw score model is labelled as the Constant and has a value of -8.939E-005. Of primary interest here are the raw (B) and standardized (Beta) coefficients, and their significance levels determined by *t* tests. The predictors are not statistically significant except for Agility in own company.

The calculated t-score for each unstandardized coefficient (coefficient divided by standard error) and their associated p-value are presented in the last two columns.

Figure 18 presents the Normal P-P Plot of Regression Standardized Residual values for Organizational reliability in own company by Agility in own company and Agility in the other company. It shows that the values are very close to the reference line, which indicates very little deviation of the expected values from the observed values.

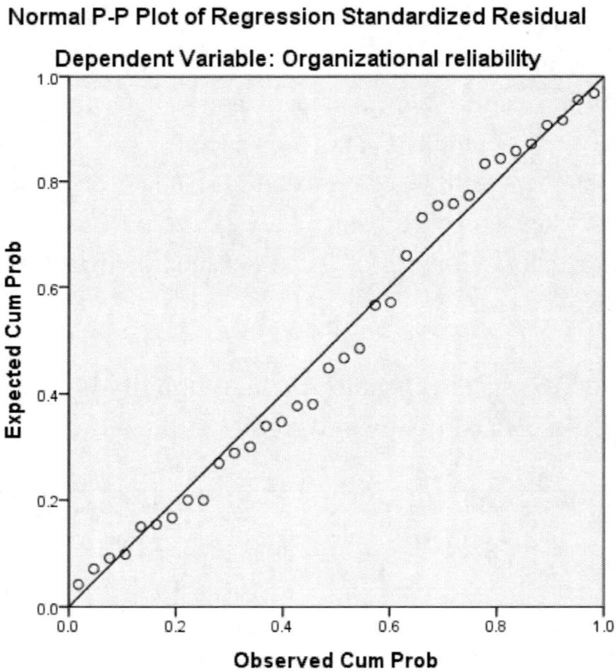

Figure no. 18. Normal P-P Plot of Regression Standardized Residual values for Organizational reliability in own company by Agility in own company and Agility in the other company.

8.3. Future Insecurity in Own Company Dependence of Cultural Differences and Respect in Own Company and Cultural Differences and Respect in the Other Company

In the Correlations for Future insecurity in own company by Cultural differences and respect in own company and Cultural differences and respect in the other company table the correlation results are divided into three major rows: the first contains the Pearson r values, the second contains the probabilities of obtaining those values if the null hypothesis was true, and the third provides sample size.

The correlation matrix table includes the correlation, p-value, and number of observations for each pair of variables in the model. For unequal number of observations for each pair, SPSS removes cases from the regression analysis which do not have complete data on all variables selected for the model. It can be noticed the lack of multicollinearity. The two predictors are not strongly related (r = -.166, p = .174). This indicates adherence to one of the assumptions of regression.

The Model Summary for Future insecurity in own company by Cultural differences and respect in own company and Cultural differences and respect in the other company table provides an overview of the results. Of primary interest are the R Square and Adjusted R Square values. It provides the Multiple Correlation (R = .411), the Multiple Correlation squared (R^2 = .169), the adjusted Multiple Correlation squared (adj. R^2 = .115), and the Standard Error of the Estimate which can be used to determine how well a regression model fits the data. The multiple correlation coefficient R can be considered to be one measure of the quality of the prediction of the dependent variable. A value of 0.411 indicates a high level of prediction.

The R2 value (also called the coefficient of determination) is the proportion of variance in the dependent variable that can be explained by the independent variables (technically, it is the proportion of variation accounted for by the regression model above and beyond the mean model).

The value of 0.169 indicates that the independent variables explain 16.9% of the variability of the dependent variable.

The multiple correlation refers to the combined correlation of each predictor with the outcome. The multiple correlation squared represents the amount of variance in the outcome which is accounted for by the predictors; here, 16.9% of the variance in Future insecurity in own company is accounted for by both Cultural differences and respect in own company and Cultural differences and respect in the other company. However, the multiple correlation squared is a bit optimistic, and therefore, the adjusted R^2 is more appropriate.

The ANOVA for Future insecurity in own company by Cultural differences and respect in own company and Cultural differences and respect in the other company table shows the test of significance of the model using an ANOVA. There are 33 (N - 1) total degrees of freedom. With two predictors, the Regression effect has two degrees of freedom. The Regression effect is statistically significant indicating that prediction of the dependent variable is accomplished better than can be done by chance.

The *F*-ratio in the ANOVA table tests whether the overall regression model is a good fit for the data. The table shows that the independent variables statistically significantly predict the dependent variable, $F\ (2, 31) = 3.152, p= 0.057$ (the regression model is a good fit of the data).

Table 35 presents the Coefficients for Future insecurity in own company by Cultural differences and respect in own company and Cultural differences and respect in the other company. The first two columns contain unstandardized (or raw score) coefficients and their standard errors. Unstandardized coefficients indicate how much the dependent variable varies with an independent variable when all other independent variables are held constant. The Constant coefficient is simply the y-intercept term for a linear best fit fine representing our fitted model. The Cultural differences and respect in own company and Cultural differences and respect in the other company unstandardized coefficients represent the weight applied to each score (for each variable) to produce new Future insecurity in own company scores along the best fit line. The unstandardized coefficients are used to build the linear regression equation one might use to predict new scores of

Future insecurity in own company using available scores of Cultural differences and respect in own company and Cultural differences and respect in own company. The equation is below:

(Future insecurity in own company) = .088 *
(Cultural differences and respect in own company) -.378 *
(Cultural differences and respect in the other company) - .064 (29)

The Standardized Coefficients, which are typically reported in social science journals (rather than the unstandardized coefficients) as a way of interpreting variable importance because, they can be directly compared (they are in the same metric). The standardized coefficients use the symbol Beta, which is the capital Greek letter β and can be interpreted as the correlation between a predictor and the outcome variable. There is no constant or y-intercept term when referring to standardized scores because, the y-intercept when graphing them is always zero. The standardization transformation results in a mean of 0 and a standard deviation of 1 for all variables so transformed.

Table 35. Coefficients for Future insecurity in own company by Cultural differences and respect in own company and Cultural differences and respect in the other company

Model		**Unstandardized Coefficients**		**Standardized Coefficients**	**t**	**Sig.**
		B	**Std. Error**	**Beta**		
1	(Constant)	-.064	.152		-.420	.677
	Cultural differences and respect in own company	.088	.150	.097	.586	.562
	Cultural differences and respect in the other company	-.378	.164	-.384	-2.310	.028

The *Y* intercept of the raw score model is labelled as the Constant and has a value of -.064. Of primary interest here are the raw (B) and standardized (Beta) coefficients, and their significance levels determined by *t* tests. The predictors are not statistically significant, except for Cultural differences and respect in the other company.

The calculated t-score for each unstandardized coefficient (coefficient divided by standard error) and their associated p-value are presented in the last two columns.

Figure 19 presents the Normal P-P Plot of Regression Standardized Residual values for Future insecurity in own company by Cultural differences and respect in own company and Cultural differences and respect in the other company. It shows that the values are very close to the reference line, which indicates very little deviation of the expected values from the observed values.

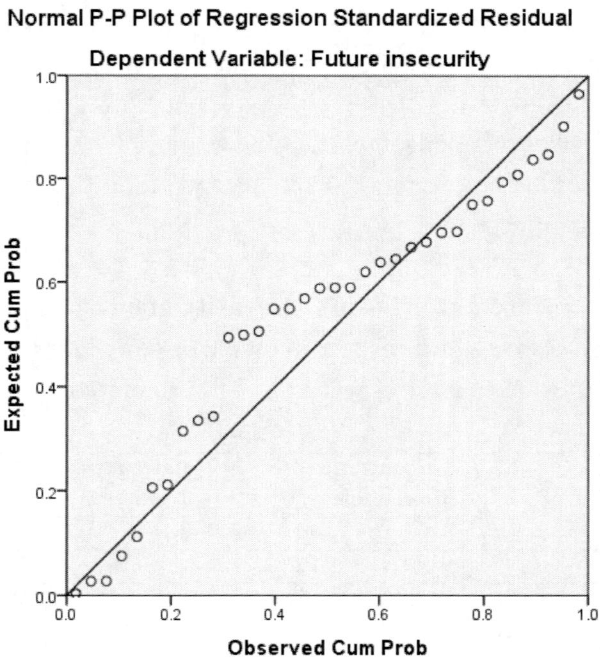

Figure 19. Normal P-P Plot of Regression Standardized Residual values for Future insecurity in own company by Cultural differences and respect in own company and Cultural differences and respect in the other company.

8.4. FUTURE INSECURITY IN THE OTHER COMPANY DEPENDENCE OF CULTURAL DIFFERENCES AND RESPECT IN OWN COMPANY AND CULTURAL DIFFERENCES AND RESPECT IN THE OTHER COMPANY

In the Correlations for Future insecurity in the other company by Cultural differences and respect in own company and Cultural differences and respect in the other company table the correlation results are divided into three major rows: the first contains the Pearson r values, the second contains the probabilities of obtaining those values if the null hypothesis was true, and the third provides sample size.

The correlation matrix table includes the correlation, p-value, and number of observations for each pair of variables in the model. For unequal number of observations for each pair, SPSS removes cases from the regression analysis which do not have complete data on all variables selected for the model. It can be noticed the lack of multicollinearity. The two predictors are not strongly related (r= -.213, p= .099). This indicates adherence to one of the assumptions of regression.

The Model Summary for Future insecurity in the other company by Cultural differences and respect in own company and Cultural differences and respect in the other company table provides an overview of the results. Of primary interest are the R Square and Adjusted R Square values. It provides the Multiple Correlation (R = .473), the Multiple Correlation squared (R^2 = .224), the adjusted Multiple Correlation squared (adj.R^2 = .179), and the Standard Error of the Estimate which can be used to determine how well a regression model fits the data.

The multiple correlation coefficient R can be considered to be one measure of the quality of the prediction of the dependent variable. A value of 0.473 indicates a high level of prediction. The R2 value (also called the coefficient of determination) is the proportion of variance in the dependent variable that can be explained by the independent variables (technically, it is the proportion of variation accounted for by the regression model above and beyond the mean model). The value of 0.224 indicates that the independent variables explain 22.4% of the variability of the dependent variable.

The multiple correlation refers to the combined correlation of each predictor with the outcome. The multiple correlation squared represents the amount of variance in the outcome which is accounted for by the predictors; here, 22.4% of the variance in Future insecurity in the other company is accounted for by both Cultural differences and respect in own company and Cultural differences and respect in the other company. However, the multiple correlation squared is a bit optimistic, and therefore, the adjusted R^2 is more appropriate.

The ANOVA for Future insecurity in the other company by Cultural differences and respect in own company and Cultural differences and respect in the other company table shows the test of significance of the model using an ANOVA. There are 37 (N - 1) total degrees of freedom. With two predictors, the Regression effect has two degrees of freedom. The Regression effect is statistically significant indicating that prediction of the dependent variable is accomplished better than can be done by chance. The F-ratio in the ANOVA table tests whether the overall regression model is a good fit for the data. The table shows that the independent variables statistically significantly predict the dependent variable, $F\ (2, 35) = 5.042$, $p= 0.012$ (the regression model is a good fit of the data).

Table 36 presents the Coefficients for Future insecurity in the other company by Cultural differences and respect in own company and Cultural differences and respect in the other company. The first two columns contain unstandardized (or raw score) coefficients and their standard errors. Unstandardized coefficients indicate how much the dependent variable varies with an independent variable when all other independent variables are held constant. The Constant coefficient is simply the y-intercept term for a linear best fit fine representing our fitted model. The Cultural differences and respect in own company and Cultural differences and respect in the other company unstandardized coefficients represent the weight applied to each score (for each variable) to produce new Future insecurity in the other company scores along the best fit line. The unstandardized coefficients are used to build the linear regression equation one might use to predict new scores of Future insecurity in the other company using available scores of Cultural differences and respect in own company and Cultural differences and respect in own company. The equation is below:

(Future insecurity in the other company) = -.456 *
(Cultural differences and respect in own company) - .248 *
(Cultural differences and respect in the other company) + .031 (30)

The Standardized Coefficients, which are typically reported in social science journals (rather than the unstandardized coefficients) as a way of interpreting variable importance because, they can be directly compared (they are in the same metric). The standardized coefficients use the symbol Beta, which is the capital Greek letter β and can be interpreted as the correlation between a predictor and the outcome variable. There is no constant or y-intercept term when referring to standardized scores because, the y-intercept when graphing them is always zero. The standardization transformation results in a mean of 0 and a standard deviation of 1 for all variables so transformed.

Table 36. Coefficients for Future insecurity in the other company by Cultural differences and respect in own company and Cultural differences and respect in the other company

Model		Unstandardized Coefficients		Standardized Coefficients	t	Sig.
		B	Std. Error	Beta		
1	(Constant)	.031	.149		.209	.835
	Cultural differences and respect in own company	-.456	.151	-.460	-3.021	.005
	Cultural differences and respect in the other company	-.248	.155	-.244	-1.601	.118

The *Y* intercept of the raw score model is labelled as the Constant and has a value of .031. Of primary interest here are the raw (B) and standardized (Beta) coefficients, and their significance levels determined by *t* tests. The predictors are statistically significant, except for Constant.

The calculated t-score for each unstandardized coefficient (coefficient divided by standard error) and their associated p-value are presented in the last two columns.

Figure 20 presents the Normal P-P Plot of Regression Standardized Residual values for Future insecurity in the other company by Cultural differences and respect in own company and Cultural differences and respect in the other company. It shows that the values are very close to the reference line, which indicates very little deviation of the expected values from the observed values.

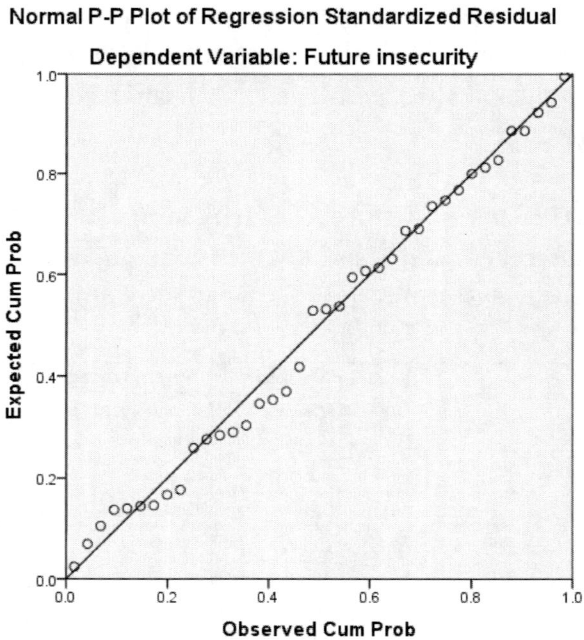

Figure 20. Normal P-P Plot of Regression Standardized Residual values for Future insecurity in the other company by Cultural differences and respect in own company and Cultural differences and respect in the other company.

8.5. Resistance Barriers in the Other Company Dependence of Group Identification in Own Company and Group Identification in the Other Company

In the Correlations for Resistance barriers in the other company by Group identification in own company and Group identification in the other company table the correlation results are divided into three major rows: the first contains the Pearson r values, the second contains the probabilities of obtaining those values if the null hypothesis was true, and the third provides sample size.

The correlation matrix table includes the correlation, p-value, and number of observations for each pair of variables in the model. For unequal number of observations for each pair, SPSS removes cases from the regression analysis which do not have complete data on all variables selected for the model. It can be noticed the lack of multicollinearity. The two predictors are not strongly related (r = .128, p = .222). This indicates adherence to one of the assumptions of regression.

The Model Summary for Resistance barriers in the other company by Group identification in own company and Group identification in the other company table provides an overview of the results. Of primary interest are the R Square and Adjusted R Square values. It provides the Multiple Correlation (R = .220), the Multiple Correlation squared (R^2 = .049), the adjusted Multiple Correlation squared (adj.R^2 = -.006), and the Standard Error of the Estimate which can be used to determine how well a regression model fits the data.

The multiple correlation coefficient R can be considered to be one measure of the quality of the prediction of the dependent variable. A value of 0.220 indicates a medium level of prediction. The R2 value (also called the coefficient of determination) is the proportion of variance in the dependent variable that can be explained by the independent variables (technically, it is the proportion of variation accounted for by the regression model above and beyond the mean model). The value of 0.049 indicates that the independent variables explain 4.9% of the variability of the dependent variable.

The multiple correlation refers to the combined correlation of each predictor with the outcome. The multiple correlation squared represents the amount of variance in the outcome which is accounted for by the predictors; here, 4.9% of the variance in Organizational functions in the post-investment stage is accounted for by both Group identification in own company and Group identification in the other company. However, the multiple correlation squared is a bit optimistic, and therefore, the adjusted R^2 is more appropriate.

The ANOVA for Resistance barriers in the other company by Group identification in own company and Group identification in the other company table shows the test of significance of the model using an ANOVA. There are 37 (N - 1) total degrees of freedom. With two predictors, the Regression effect has two degrees of freedom. The Regression effect is statistically significant indicating that prediction of the dependent variable is accomplished better than can be done by chance. The *F*-ratio in the **ANOVA** table tests whether the overall regression model is a good fit for the data. The table shows that the independent variables statistically significantly do not predict the dependent variable, F (2, 35) = .892, $p = 0.419$ (the regression model is not a good fit of the data).

Table 37 presents the Coefficients for Resistance barriers in the other company by Group identification in own company and Group identification in the other company. The first two columns contain unstandardized (or raw score) coefficients and their standard errors. Unstandardized coefficients indicate how much the dependent variable varies with an independent variable when all other independent variables are held constant. The Constant coefficient is simply the y-intercept term for a linear best fit fine representing our fitted model. The Group identification in own company and Group identification in the other company unstandardized coefficients represent the weight applied to each score (for each variable) to produce new Resistance barriers in the other company scores along the best fit line. The unstandardized coefficients are used to build the linear regression equation one might use to predict new scores of Resistance barriers in the other company using available scores of Group identification in own company and Group identification in the other company. The equation is below:

(Resistance barriers in the other company) = -.146 *
(Group identification in own company) - .160 *
(Group identification in the other company) + .051 (31)

The Standardized Coefficients, which are typically reported in social science journals (rather than the unstandardized coefficients) as a way of interpreting variable importance because, they can be directly compared (they are in the same metric). The standardized coefficients use the symbol Beta, which is the capital Greek letter β and can be interpreted as the correlation between a predictor and the outcome variable. There is no constant or y-intercept term when referring to standardized scores because, the y-intercept when graphing them is always zero. The standardization transformation results in a mean of 0 and a standard deviation of 1 for all variables so transformed.

Table 37. Coefficients for Resistance barriers in the other company by Group identification in own company and Group identification in the other company

Model		**Unstandardized Coefficients**		**Standardized Coefficients**	**t**	**Sig.**
		B	**Std. Error**	**Beta**		
1	(Constant)	.051	.166		.309	.759
	Group identification in own company	-.146	.189	-.128	-.772	.445
	Group identification in the other company	-.160	.163	-.163	-.983	.333

The *Y* intercept of the raw score model is labelled as the Constant and has a value of .051. Of primary interest here are the raw (B) and standardized (Beta) coefficients, and their significance levels determined by *t* tests. The predictors are not statistically significant.

The calculated t-score for each unstandardized coefficient (coefficient divided by standard error) and their associated p-value are presented in the last two columns.

Figure 21 presents the Normal P-P Plot of Regression Standardized Residual values for Resistance barriers in the other company by Group identification in own company and Group identification in the other company. It shows that the values are very close to the reference line, which indicates very little deviation of the expected values from the observed values.

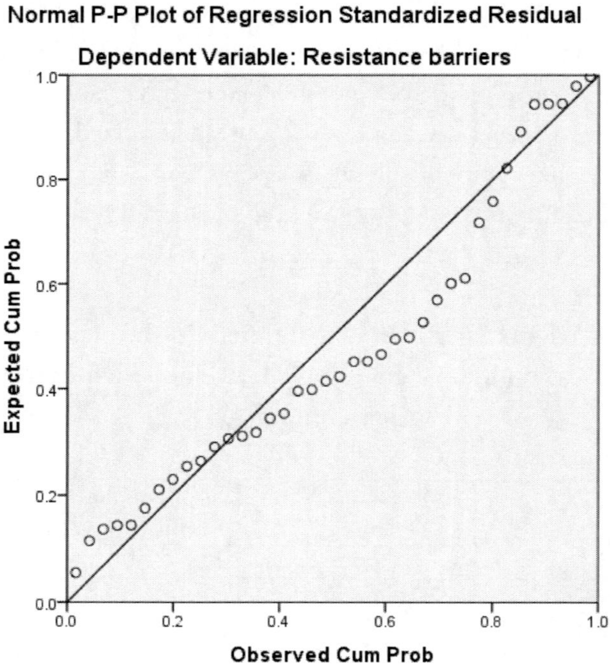

Figure 21. Normal P-P Plot of Regression Standardized Residual values for Resistance barriers in the other company by Group identification in own company and Group identification in the other company.

8.6. Resistance Barriers in Own Company Dependence of Group Identification in Own Company and Group Identification in the Other Company

In the Correlations for Resistance barriers in own company by Group identification in own company and Group identification in the other company table the correlation results are divided into three major rows: the first contains the Pearson r values, the second contains the probabilities of obtaining those values if the null hypothesis was true, and the third provides sample size.

The correlation matrix table includes the correlation, p-value, and number of observations for each pair of variables in the model. For unequal number of observations for each pair, SPSS removes cases from the regression analysis which do not have complete data on all variables selected for the model. It can be noticed the lack of multicollinearity. The two predictors are not strongly related (r = .301, p = .042). This indicates adherence to one of the assumptions of regression.

The Model Summary for Resistance barriers in own company by Group identification in own company and Group identification in the other company table provides an overview of the results. Of primary interest are the R Square and Adjusted R Square values. It provides the Multiple Correlation (R = .322), the Multiple Correlation squared (R^2 = .104), the adjusted Multiple Correlation squared (adj.R^2 = .046), and the Standard Error of the Estimate which can be used to determine how well a regression model fits the data.

The multiple correlation coefficient R can be considered to be one measure of the quality of the prediction of the dependent variable. A value of 0.322 indicates a medium level of prediction. The R2 value (also called the coefficient of determination) is the proportion of variance in the dependent variable that can be explained by the independent variables (technically, it is the proportion of variation accounted for by the regression model above and beyond the mean model). The value of 0.104 indicates that the independent variables explain 10.4% of the variability of the dependent variable.

The multiple correlation refers to the combined correlation of each predictor with the outcome. The multiple correlation squared represents the amount of variance in the outcome which is accounted for by the predictors; here, 10.4% of the variance in Resistance barriers in own company is accounted for by both Group identification in own company, Group identification in the other company. However, the multiple correlation squared is a bit optimistic, and therefore, the adjusted R^2 is more appropriate.

The ANOVA for Resistance barriers in own company by Group identification in own company and Group identification in the other company table shows the test of significance of the model using an ANOVA. There are 33 (N - 1) total degrees of freedom. With two predictors, the Regression effect has two degrees of freedom. The Regression effect is statistically significant indicating that prediction of the dependent variable is accomplished better than can be done by chance.

The *F*-ratio in the ANOVA table tests whether the overall regression model is a good fit for the data. The table shows that the independent variables statistically significantly predict the dependent variable, $F\,(2, 31) = 1.795$, $p = 0.183$ (the regression model is a good fit of the data).

Table 38 presents the Coefficients for Resistance barriers in own company by Group identification in own company and Group identification in the other company. The first two columns contain unstandardized (or raw score) coefficients and their standard errors. Unstandardized coefficients indicate how much the dependent variable varies with an independent variable when all other independent variables are held constant. The Constant coefficient is simply the y-intercept term for a linear best fit fine representing our fitted model. The Group identification in own company and Group identification in the other company unstandardized coefficients represent the weight applied to each score (for each variable) to produce new Resistance barriers in own company scores along the best fit line. The unstandardized coefficients are used to build the linear regression equation one might use to predict new scores of Resistance barriers in own company using available scores of Group identification in own company and Group identification in the other company. The equation is below:

(Resistance barriers in own company) -.369 *
(Group identification in own company) -.072 *
(Group identification in the other company) + .033 (32)

The Standardized Coefficients, which are typically reported in social science journals (rather than the unstandardized coefficients) as a way of interpreting variable importance because, they can be directly compared (they are in the same metric). The standardized coefficients use the symbol Beta, which is the capital Greek letter β and can be interpreted as the correlation between a predictor and the outcome variable. There is no constant or y-intercept term when referring to standardized scores because, the y-intercept when graphing them is always zero. The standardization transformation results in a mean of 0 and a standard deviation of 1 for all variables so transformed.

Table 38. Coefficients for Resistance barriers in own company by Group identification in own company and Group identification in the other company

Model		Unstandardized Coefficients		Standardized Coefficients	t	Sig.
		B	Std. Error	Beta		
1	(Constant)	.033	.178		.183	.856
	Group identification in own company	-.369	.223	-.295	-1.653	.108
	Group identification in the other company	-.072	.186	-.069	-.386	.702

The *Y* intercept of the raw score model is labelled as the Constant and has a value of .033. Of primary interest here are the raw (B) and standardized (Beta) coefficients, and their significance levels determined by *t* tests. The predictors are not statistically significant, except for Group identification in own company.

The calculated t-score for each unstandardized coefficient (coefficient divided by standard error) and their associated p-value are presented in the last two columns.

Figure 22 presents the Normal P-P Plot of Regression Standardized Residual values for Resistance barriers in own company by Group identification in own company and Group identification in the other company. It shows that the values are very close to the reference line, which indicates very little deviation of the expected values from the observed values.

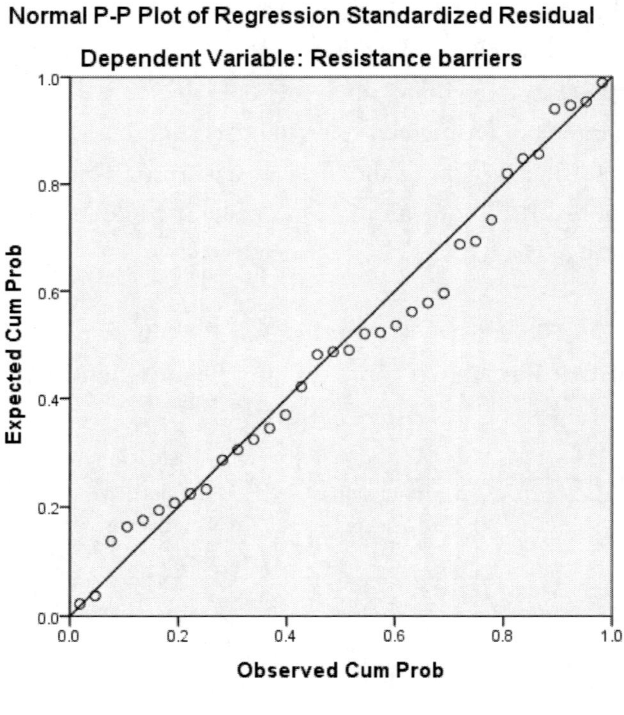

Figure 22. Normal P-P Plot of Regression Standardized Residual values for Resistance barriers in own company by Group identification in own company and Group identification in the other company.

8.7. Organizational Distrust in the Other Company Dependence of Agility in Own Company and Agility in the Other Company

In the Correlations for Organizational distrust in the other company by Agility in own company and Agility in the other company table the correlation results are divided into three major rows: the first contains the Pearson r values, the second contains the probabilities of obtaining those values if the null hypothesis was true, and the third provides sample size.

The correlation matrix table includes the correlation, p-value, and number of observations for each pair of variables in the model. For unequal number of observations for each pair, SPSS removes cases from the regression analysis which do not have complete data on all variables selected for the model. It can be noticed the lack of multicollinearity. The two predictors are not strongly related (r = .070, p = .338). This indicates adherence to one of the assumptions of regression.

The Model Summary for Organizational distrust in the other company by Agility in own company and Agility in the other company table provides an overview of the results. Of primary interest are the R Square and Adjusted R Square values. It provides the Multiple Correlation (R = .480), the Multiple Correlation squared (R^2 = .231), the adjusted Multiple Correlation squared (adj.R^2 = .187), and the Standard Error of the Estimate which can be used to determine how well a regression model fits the data.

The multiple correlation coefficient R can be considered to be one measure of the quality of the prediction of the dependent variable. A value of 0.480 indicates a high level of prediction. The R2 value (also called the coefficient of determination) is the proportion of variance in the dependent variable that can be explained by the independent variables (technically, it is the proportion of variation accounted for by the regression model above and beyond the mean model). The value of 0.231 indicates that the independent variables explain 23.1% of the variability of the dependent variable.

The multiple correlation refers to the combined correlation of each predictor with the outcome. The multiple correlation squared represents the amount of variance in the outcome which is accounted for by the predictors; here, 23.1% of the variance in Organizational distrust in the other company is accounted for by both Agility in own company, Agility in the other company and respect in the other company. However, the multiple correlation squared is a bit optimistic, and therefore, the adjusted R^2 is more appropriate.

The ANOVA for Organizational distrust in the other company by Agility in own company and Agility in the other company table shows the test of significance of the model using an ANOVA. There are 37 (N - 1) total degrees of freedom. With two predictors, the Regression effect has two degrees of freedom. The Regression effect is statistically significant indicating that prediction of the dependent variable is accomplished better than can be done by chance.

The *F*-ratio in the ANOVA table tests whether the overall regression model is a good fit for the data. The table shows that the independent variables statistically significantly predict the dependent variable, $F(2, 35) = 5.249$, $p = 0.010$ (the regression model is a good fit of the data).

Table 39 presents the Coefficients for Organizational distrust in the other company by Agility in own company and Agility in the other company. The first two columns contain unstandardized (or raw score) coefficients and their standard errors. Unstandardized coefficients indicate how much the dependent variable varies with an independent variable when all other independent variables are held constant. The Constant coefficient is simply the y-intercept term for a linear best fit fine representing our fitted model. The Agility in own company and Agility in the other company unstandardized coefficients represent the weight applied to each score (for each variable) to produce new Organizational distrust in the other company scores along the best fit line. The unstandardized coefficients are used to build the linear regression equation one might use to predict new scores of Organizational distrust in the other company using available scores of Agility in own company and Agility in the other company. The equation is below:

(Organizational distrust in the other company) = -.152 *
(Agility in own company) + .460 *
(Agility in the other company) + .016 (33)

Table 39. Coefficients for Organizational distrust in the other company by Agility in own company and Agility in the other company

Model		Unstandardized Coefficients		Standardized Coefficients	t	Sig.
		B	Std. Error	Beta		
1	(Constant)	.016	.153		.104	.918
	Agility in own company	-.152	.154	-.146	-.986	.331
	Agility in the other company	.460	.146	.468	3.148	.003

The Standardized Coefficients, which are typically reported in social science journals (rather than the unstandardized coefficients) as a way of interpreting variable importance because, they can be directly compared (they are in the same metric). The standardized coefficients use the symbol Beta, which is the capital Greek letter β and can be interpreted as the correlation between a predictor and the outcome variable. There is no constant or y-intercept term when referring to standardized scores because, the y-intercept when graphing them is always zero. The standardization transformation results in a mean of 0 and a standard deviation of 1 for all variables so transformed.

The *Y* intercept of the raw score model is labelled as the Constant and has a value of .016. Of primary interest here are the raw (B) and standardized (Beta) coefficients, and their significance levels determined by *t* tests. The predictors are not statistically significant, except for Agility in the other company.

The calculated t-score for each unstandardized coefficient (coefficient divided by standard error) and their associated p-value are presented in the last two columns.

Figure 23. presents the Normal P-P Plot of Regression Standardized Residual values for Organizational distrust in the other company by Agility in own company and Agility in the other company. It shows that the values are very close to the reference line, which indicates very little deviation of the expected values from the observed values.

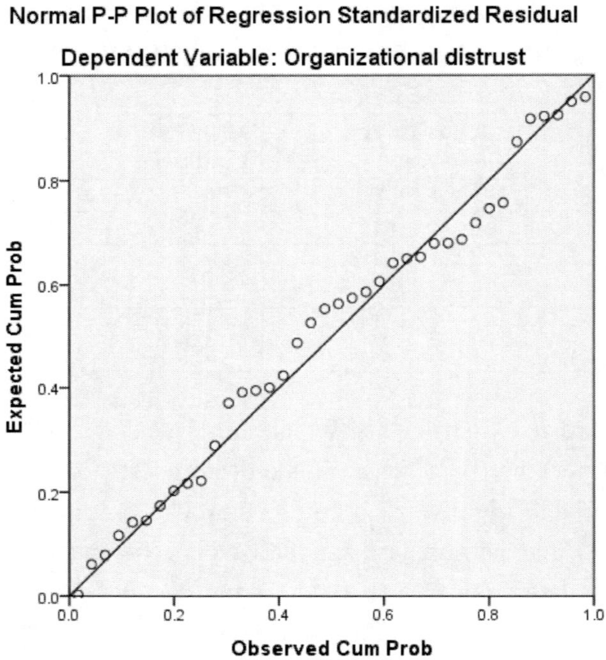

Figure 23. Normal P-P Plot of Regression Standardized Residual values for Organizational distrust in the other company by Agility in own company and Agility in the other company.

8.8. Organizational Distrust in Own Company Dependence of Agility in Own Company and Agility in the Other Company

In the Correlations for Organizational distrust in own company by Agility in own company and Agility in the other company table the correlation results are divided into three major rows: the first contains the

Pearson r values, the second contains the probabilities of obtaining those values if the null hypothesis was true, and the third provides sample size.

The correlation matrix table includes the correlation, p-value, and number of observations for each pair of variables in the model. For unequal number of observations for each pair, SPSS removes cases from the regression analysis which do not have complete data on all variables selected for the model. It can be noticed the lack of multicollinearity. The two predictors are not strongly related (r = .053, p = .383). This indicates adherence to one of the assumptions of regression.

The Model Summary for Organizational distrust in own company by Agility in own company and Agility in the other company table provides an overview of the results. Of primary interest are the R Square and Adjusted R Square values. It provides the Multiple Correlation (R = .241), the Multiple Correlation squared (R^2 = .058), the adjusted Multiple Correlation squared (adj.R^2 = -.003), and the Standard Error of the Estimate which can be used to determine how well a regression model fits the data.

The multiple correlation coefficient R can be considered to be one measure of the quality of the prediction of the dependent variable. A value of 0.241 indicates a medium level of prediction. The R2 value (also called the coefficient of determination) is the proportion of variance in the dependent variable that can be explained by the independent variables (technically, it is the proportion of variation accounted for by the regression model above and beyond the mean model). The value of 0.058 indicates that the independent variables explain 5.8% of the variability of the dependent variable.

The multiple correlation refers to the combined correlation of each predictor with the outcome. The multiple correlation squared represents the amount of variance in the outcome which is accounted for by the predictors; here, 5.8% of the variance in Organizational distrust in own company is accounted for by both Agility in own company and Agility in the other company. However, the multiple correlation squared is a bit optimistic, and therefore, the adjusted R^2 is more appropriate.

The ANOVA for Organizational distrust in own company by Agility in own company and Agility in the other company table shows the test of significance of the model using an ANOVA. There are 33 (N - 1) total degrees of freedom. With two predictors, the Regression effect has two degrees of freedom. The Regression effect is statistically significant indicating that prediction of the dependent variable is accomplished better than can be done by chance.

The *F*-ratio in the ANOVA table tests whether the overall regression model is a good fit for the data. The table shows that the independent variables statistically significantly do not predict the dependent variable, $F(2, 31) = .953, p= 0.396$ (the regression model is not a good fit of the data).

Table 40 presents the Coefficients for Organizational distrust in own company by Agility in own company and Agility in the other company. The first two columns contain unstandardized (or raw score) coefficients and their standard errors. Unstandardized coefficients indicate how much the dependent variable varies with an independent variable when all other independent variables are held constant. The Constant coefficient is simply the y-intercept term for a linear best fit fine representing our fitted model. The Agility in own company and Agility in the other company unstandardized coefficients represent the weight applied to each score (for each variable) to produce new Organizational distrust in own company scores along the best fit line. The unstandardized coefficients are used to build the linear regression equation one might use to predict new scores of Organizational distrust in own company using available scores of Agility in own company and Agility in the other company. The equation is below:

$$\begin{aligned}&(\text{Organizational distrust in own company}) = -.232 * \\&(\text{Agility in own company}) + .045 * \\&(\text{Agility in the other company}) + .083 \qquad (34)\end{aligned}$$

The Standardized Coefficients, which are typically reported in social science journals (rather than the unstandardized coefficients) as a way of interpreting variable importance because, they can be directly compared (they are in the same metric). The standardized coefficients use the symbol Beta, which is the capital Greek letter β and can be interpreted as the correlation between a predictor and the outcome variable. There is no constant or y-intercept term when referring to standardized scores because, the y-intercept when graphing them is always zero. The standardization transformation results in a mean of 0 and a standard deviation of 1 for all variables so transformed.

Table 40. Coefficients for Organizational distrust in own company by Agility in own company and Agility in the other company

Model		Unstandardized Coefficients		Standardized Coefficients	t	Sig.
		B	Std. Error	Beta		
1	(Constant)	.083	.172		.482	.633
	Agility in own company	-.232	.170	-.239	-1.369	.181
	Agility in the other company	.045	.175	.045	.256	.799

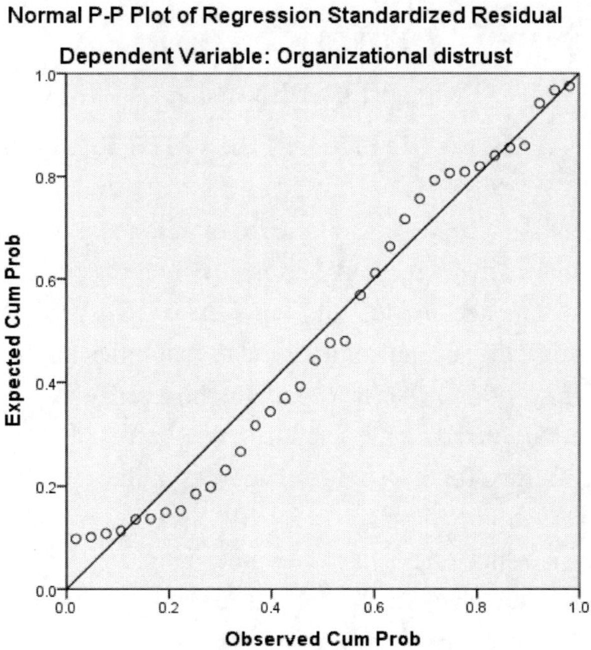

Figure 24. Normal P-P Plot of Regression Standardized Residual values for Organizational distrust in own company by Agility in own company and Agility in the other company.

The *Y* intercept of the raw score model is labelled as the Constant and has a value of .083. Of primary interest here are the raw (B) and standardized (Beta) coefficients, and their significance levels determined by *t* tests. The predictors are not statistically significant, except for Agility in own company.

The calculated t-score for each unstandardized coefficient (coefficient divided by standard error) and their associated p-value are presented in the last two columns.

Figure 24 presents the Normal P-P Plot of Regression Standardized Residual values for Organizational distrust in own company by Agility in own company and Agility in the other company The Normal P-P Plot of Regression Standardized Residual values shows that the values are very close to the reference line, which indicates very little deviation of the expected values from the observed values.

8.9. Managers' Degree of Autonomy, Impact on M&A Outcome Dependence of Agility in Own Company and Agility in the Other Company

In the Correlations for Managers' degree of autonomy, impact on M&A outcome by Agility in own company and Agility in the other company table the correlation results are divided into three major rows: the first contains the Pearson r values, the second contains the probabilities of obtaining those values if the null hypothesis was true, and the third provides sample size.

The correlation matrix table includes the correlation, p-value, and number of observations for each pair of variables in the model. For unequal number of observations for each pair, SPSS removes cases from the regression analysis which do not have complete data on all variables selected for the model. It can be noticed the lack of multicollinearity. The two predictors are not strongly related ($r = .077$, $p = .318$). This indicates adherence to one of the assumptions of regression.

The Model Summary for Managers' degree of autonomy, impact on M&A outcome by Agility in own company and Agility in the other company table provides an overview of the results. Of primary interest are the R

Square and Adjusted R Square values. It provides the Multiple Correlation (R = .439), the Multiple Correlation squared (R^2 = .193), the adjusted Multiple Correlation squared (adj.R^2 = .149), and the Standard Error of the Estimate which can be used to determine how well a regression model fits the data.

The multiple correlation coefficient R can be considered to be one measure of the quality of the prediction of the dependent variable. A value of 0.439 indicates a high level of prediction. The R2 value (also called the coefficient of determination) is the proportion of variance in the dependent variable that can be explained by the independent variables (technically, it is the proportion of variation accounted for by the regression model above and beyond the mean model). The value of 0.193 indicates that the independent variables explain 19.3% of the variability of the dependent variable.

The multiple correlation refers to the combined correlation of each predictor with the outcome. The multiple correlation squared represents the amount of variance in the outcome which is accounted for by the predictors; here, 19.3% of the variance in Managers' degree of autonomy, impact on M&A outcome is accounted for by both Agility in own company and Agility in the other company. However, the multiple correlation squared is a bit optimistic, and therefore, the adjusted R^2 is more appropriate.

The ANOVA for Managers' degree of autonomy, impact on M&A outcome by Agility in own company and Agility in the other company table shows the test of significance of the model using an ANOVA. There are 39 (N - 1) total degrees of freedom. With two predictors, the Regression effect has two degrees of freedom. The Regression effect is statistically significant indicating that prediction of the dependent variable is accomplished better than can be done by chance.

The F-ratio in the ANOVA table tests whether the overall regression model is a good fit for the data. The table shows that the independent variables statistically significantly predict the dependent variable, $F(2, 37) = 4.414$, $p = 0.019$ (the regression model is a good fit of the data).

Table 41 presents the Coefficients for Managers' degree of autonomy, impact on M&A outcome by Agility in own company and Agility in the other company. The first two columns contain unstandardized (or raw score) coefficients and their standard errors. Unstandardized coefficients indicate how much the dependent variable varies with an independent variable when all other independent variables are held constant. The Constant coefficient is simply the y-intercept term for a linear best fit fine representing our fitted model. The Agility in own company and Agility in the other company unstandardized coefficients represent the weight applied to each score (for each variable) to produce new Managers' degree of autonomy, impact on M&A outcome scores along the best fit line. The unstandardized coefficients are used to build the linear regression equation one might use to predict new scores of Managers' degree of autonomy, impact on M&A outcome using available scores of Agility in own company and Agility in the other company. The equation is below:

$$\text{(Managers' degree of autonomy, impact on M\&A outcome)} = .100 * \text{(Agility in own company)} + .346 * \text{(Agility in the other company)} + 3.663 \quad (35)$$

Table 41. Coefficients for Managers' degree of autonomy, impact on M&A outcome by Agility in own company and Agility in the other company

Model		Unstandardized Coefficients		Standardized Coefficients	t	Sig.
		B	Std. Error	Beta		
1	(Constant)	3.663	.126		29.052	.000
	Agility in own company	.100	.126	.117	.787	.436
	Agility in the other company	.346	.124	.414	2.796	.008

The Standardized Coefficients, which are typically reported in social science journals (rather than the unstandardized coefficients) as a way of interpreting variable importance because, they can be directly compared (they are in the same metric). The standardized coefficients use the symbol Beta, which is the capital Greek letter β and can be interpreted as the correlation between a predictor and the outcome variable. There is no constant or y-intercept term when referring to standardized scores because, the y-intercept when graphing them is always zero. The standardization transformation results in a mean of 0 and a standard deviation of 1 for all variables so transformed.

The *Y* intercept of the raw score model is labelled as the Constant and has a value of 3.663. Of primary interest here are the raw (B) and standardized (Beta) coefficients, and their significance levels determined by *t* tests. The predictors are statistically significant, except for Agility in own company.

The calculated t-score for each unstandardized coefficient (coefficient divided by standard error) and their associated p-value are presented in the last two columns.

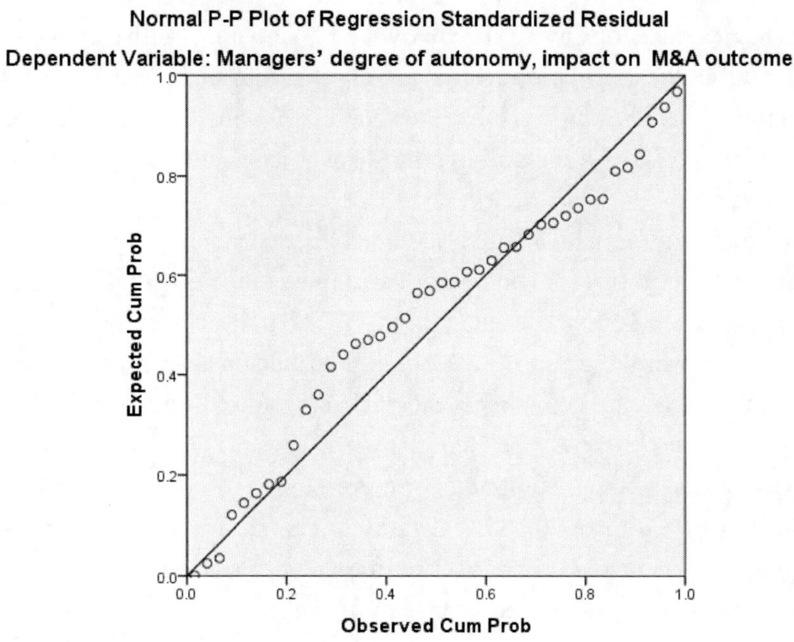

Figure 25. Normal P-P Plot of Regression Standardized Residual values for Managers' degree of autonomy, impact on M&A outcome by Agility in own company and Agility in the other company.

Figure 25. Normal P-P Plot of Regression Standardized Residual values for Managers' degree of autonomy, impact on M&A outcome by Agility in own company and Agility in the other company. It shows that the values are very close to the reference line, which indicates very little deviation of the expected values from the observed values.

8.10. Organizational Change Resistance, Impact on Top Management's Decisions Dependence of Agility in Own Company and Agility in the Other Company

In the Correlations for Organizational change resistance, impact on top management's decisions by Agility in own company and Agility in the other company table the correlation results are divided into three major rows: the first contains the Pearson r values, the second contains the probabilities of obtaining those values if the null hypothesis was true, and the third provides sample size.

The correlation matrix table includes the correlation, p-value, and number of observations for each pair of variables in the model. For unequal number of observations for each pair, SPSS removes cases from the regression analysis which do not have complete data on all variables selected for the model. It can be noticed the lack of multicollinearity. The two predictors are not strongly related ($r = .077$, $p = .318$). This indicates adherence to one of the assumptions of regression.

The Model Summary for Organizational change resistance, impact on top management's decisions by Agility in own company and Agility in the other company table provides an overview of the results. Of primary interest are the R Square and Adjusted R Square values. It provides the Multiple Correlation ($R = .261$), the Multiple Correlation squared ($R^2 = .068$), the adjusted Multiple Correlation squared (adj.$R^2 = .018$), and the Standard Error of the Estimate which can be used to determine how well a regression model fits the data.

The multiple correlation coefficient R can be considered to be one measure of the quality of the prediction of the dependent variable. A value of 0.261 indicates a medium level of prediction. The R2 value (also called the coefficient of determination) is the proportion of variance in the dependent variable that can be explained by the independent variables (technically, it is the proportion of variation accounted for by the regression model above and beyond the mean model). The value of 0.068 indicates that the independent variables explain 6.8% of the variability of the dependent variable.

The multiple correlation refers to the combined correlation of each predictor with the outcome. The multiple correlation squared represents the amount of variance in the outcome which is accounted for by the predictors; here, 6.8% of the variance in Organizational change resistance, impact on top management's decisions is accounted for by both Agility in own company and Agility in the other company. However, the multiple correlation squared is a bit optimistic, and therefore, the adjusted R^2 is more appropriate.

The ANOVA for Organizational change resistance, impact on top management's decisions by Agility in own company and Agility in the other company table shows the test of significance of the model using an ANOVA. There are 39 (N - 1) total degrees of freedom. With two predictors, the Regression effect has two degrees of freedom. The Regression effect is statistically significant indicating that prediction of the dependent variable is accomplished better than can be done by chance. The *F*-ratio in the ANOVA table tests whether the overall regression model is a good fit for the data. The table shows that the independent variables statistically significantly do not predict the dependent variable, F (2, 37) = 1.350, $p = 0.272$ (the regression model is not a good fit of the data).

Table 42 presents the Coefficients for Organizational change resistance, impact on top management's decisions by Agility in own company and Agility in the other company. The first two columns contain unstandardized (or raw score) coefficients and their standard errors. Unstandardized coefficients indicate how much the dependent variable varies with an independent variable when all other independent variables are held constant.

The Constant coefficient is simply the y-intercept term for a linear best fit fine representing our fitted model. The Agility in own company and Agility in the other company unstandardized coefficients represent the weight applied to each score (for each variable) to produce new Organizational change resistance, impact on top management's decisions scores along the best fit line. The unstandardized coefficients are used to build the linear regression equation one might use to predict new scores of Organizational change resistance, impact on top management's decisions using available scores of Agility in own company and Agility in the other company. The equation is below:

$$\text{(Organizational change resistance, impact on top management's decisions)} = .216 * \text{(Agility in own company)} + .070 * \text{(Agility in the other company)} + 3.177 \quad (36)$$

The Standardized Coefficients, which are typically reported in social science journals (rather than the unstandardized coefficients) as a way of interpreting variable importance because, they can be directly compared (they are in the same metric). The standardized coefficients use the symbol Beta, which is the capital Greek letter β and can be interpreted as the correlation between a predictor and the outcome variable. There is no constant or y-intercept term when referring to standardized scores because, the y-intercept when graphing them is always zero. The standardization transformation results in a mean of 0 and a standard deviation of 1 for all variables so transformed.

The *Y* intercept of the raw score model is labelled as the Constant and has a value of 3.177. Of primary interest here are the raw (B) and standardized (Beta) coefficients, and their significance levels determined by *t* tests. The predictors are statistically significant, except for Agility in the other company.

The calculated t-score for each unstandardized coefficient (coefficient divided by standard error) and their associated p-value are presented in the last two columns.

Table 42. Coefficients for Organizational change resistance, impact on top management's decisions by Agility in own company and Agility in the other company

Model		Unstandardized Coefficients		Standardized Coefficients	t	Sig.
		B	Std. Error	Beta		
1	(Constant)	3.177	.142		22.438	.000
	Agility in own company	.216	.142	.242	1.520	.137
	Agility in the other company	.070	.139	.081	.507	.615

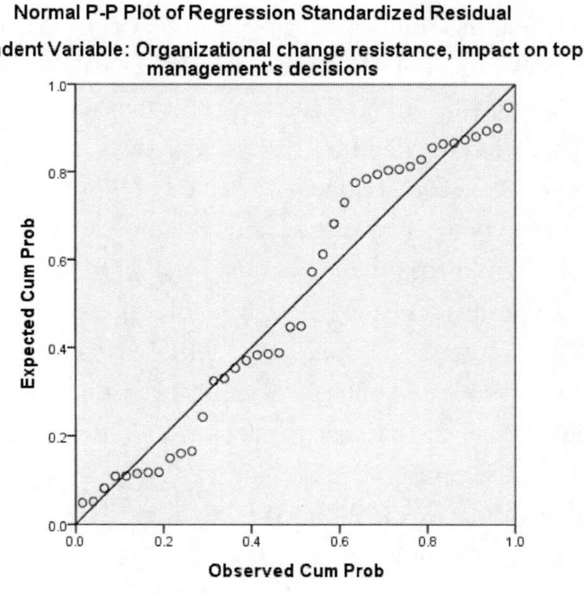

Figure no. 26. Normal P-P Plot of Regression Standardized Residual values for Organizational change resistance, impact on top management's decisions by Agility in own company and Agility in the other company.

Figure 26 presents the Normal P-P Plot of Regression Standardized Residual values for Organizational change resistance, impact on top management's decisions by Agility in own company and Agility in the other company. It shows that the values are very close to the reference line, which indicates very little deviation of the expected values from the observed values.

8.11. Top Management's Decisions, Impact on the Integration Process Outcome Dependence of Cultural Differences and Respect in Own Company and Cultural Differences and Respect in the Other Company

In the Correlations for Top management's decisions, impact on the integration process outcome by Cultural differences and respect in own company and Cultural differences and respect in the other company table the correlation results are divided into three major rows: the first contains the Pearson r values, the second contains the probabilities of obtaining those values if the null hypothesis was true, and the third provides sample size.

The correlation matrix table includes the correlation, p-value, and number of observations for each pair of variables in the model. For unequal number of observations for each pair, SPSS removes cases from the regression analysis which do not have complete data on all variables selected for the model. It can be noticed the lack of multicollinearity. The two predictors are not strongly related (r = -.193, p = .116). This indicates adherence to one of the assumptions of regression.

The Model Summary for Top management's decisions, impact on the integration process outcome by Cultural differences and respect in own company and Cultural differences and respect in the other company table provides an overview of the results. Of primary interest are the R Square and Adjusted R Square values. It provides the Multiple Correlation (R = .284), the Multiple Correlation squared (R^2 = .081), the adjusted Multiple Correlation squared (adj.R^2 = .031), and the Standard Error of the Estimate which can be used to determine how well a regression model fits the data.

The multiple correlation coefficient R can be considered to be one measure of the quality of the prediction of the dependent variable. A value of 0.284 indicates a medium level of prediction. The R2 value (also called the coefficient of determination) is the proportion of variance in the dependent variable that can be explained by the independent variables (technically, it is the proportion of variation accounted for by the regression model above and beyond the mean model). The value of 0.081 indicates that the independent variables explain 8.1% of the variability of the dependent variable.

The multiple correlation refers to the combined correlation of each predictor with the outcome. The multiple correlation squared represents the amount of variance in the outcome which is accounted for by the predictors; here, 8.1% of the variance in Top management's decisions, impact on the integration process outcome is accounted for by both Cultural differences and respect in own company and Cultural differences and respect in the other company. However, the multiple correlation squared is a bit optimistic, and therefore, the adjusted R^2 is more appropriate.

The ANOVA for Top management's decisions, impact on the integration process outcome by Cultural differences and respect in own company and Cultural differences and respect in the other company table shows the test of significance of the model using an ANOVA. There are 39 (N - 1) total degrees of freedom. With two predictors, the Regression effect has two degrees of freedom. The Regression effect is statistically significant indicating that prediction of the dependent variable is accomplished better than can be done by chance. The *F*-ratio in the ANOVA table tests whether the overall regression model is a good fit for the data. The table shows that the independent variables statistically significantly do not predict the dependent variable, $F(2, 37) = 1.626$, $p = 0.210$ (the regression model is not a good fit of the data).

Table 43 presents the Coefficients for Top management's decisions, impact on the integration process outcome by Cultural differences and respect in own company and Cultural differences and respect in the other company. The first two columns contain unstandardized (or raw score) coefficients and their standard errors. Unstandardized coefficients indicate how much the dependent variable varies with an independent variable when all other independent variables are held constant. The Constant coefficient is simply the y-intercept term for a linear best fit fine representing our fitted model. The Cultural differences and respect in own company and Cultural differences and respect in the other company unstandardized coefficients represent the weight applied to each score (for each variable) to produce new Top management's decisions, impact on the integration process outcome scores along the best fit line. The unstandardized coefficients are used to build the linear regression equation one might use to predict new scores of Top management's decisions, impact on the integration process outcome using available scores of Cultural differences and respect in own company and Cultural differences and respect in own company. The equation is below:

(Top management's decisions, impact on the integration process outcome) = -.230 *
(Cultural differences and respect in own company) - .129 *
(Cultural differences and respect in the other company) + 4.001 (37)

Table 43. Coefficients for top management's decisions, impact on the integration process outcome by cultural differences and respect in own company and cultural differences and respect in the other company

Model		Unstandardized Coefficients		Standardized Coefficients	t	Sig.
		B	Std. Error	Beta		
1	(Constant)	4.001	.132		30.306	.000
	Cultural differences and respect in own company	-.230	.136	-.272	-1.696	.098
	Cultural differences and respect in the other company	-.129	.139	-.149	-.930	.358

The Standardized Coefficients, which are typically reported in social science journals (rather than the unstandardized coefficients) as a way of interpreting variable importance because, they can be directly compared (they are in the same metric). The standardized coefficients use the symbol Beta, which is the capital Greek letter β and can be interpreted as the correlation between a predictor and the outcome variable. There is no constant or y-intercept term when referring to standardized scores because, the y-intercept when graphing them is always zero. The standardization transformation results in a mean of 0 and a standard deviation of 1 for all variables so transformed.

The *Y* intercept of the raw score model is labelled as the Constant and has a value of 4.001. Of primary interest here are the raw (B) and standardized (Beta) coefficients, and their significance levels determined by *t* tests. The predictors are not statistically significant, except for Cultural differences and respect in the other company.

The calculated t-score for each unstandardized coefficient (coefficient divided by standard error) and their associated p-value are presented in the last two columns.

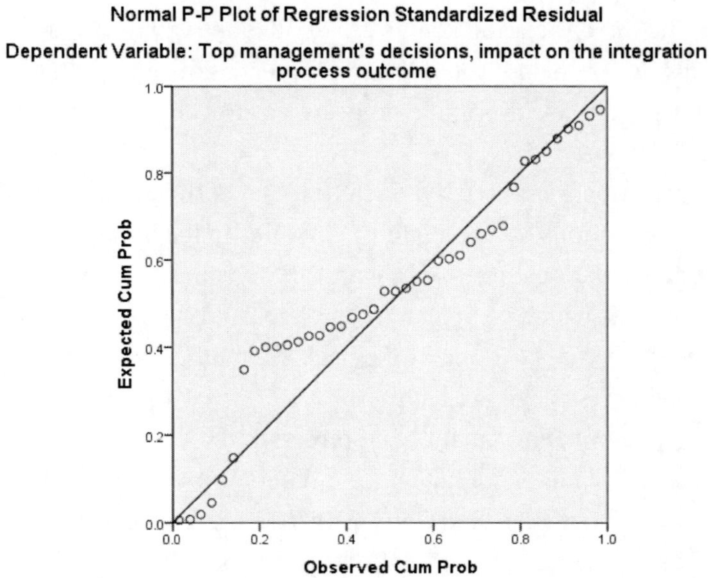

Figure no. 27. Normal P-P Plot of Regression Standardized Residual values for Top management's decisions, impact on the integration process outcome by Cultural differences and respect in own company and Cultural differences and respect in the other company.

Figure 27 presents the Normal P-P Plot of Regression Standardized Residual values for Top management's decisions, impact on the integration process outcome by Cultural differences and respect in own company and Cultural differences and respect in the other company. It shows that the values are very close to the reference line, which indicates very little deviation of the expected values from the observed values.

8.12. Integration Outcome Dependence of Cultural Differences and Respect in Own Company and Cultural Differences and Respect in the Other Company

In the Correlations for Integration outcome by Cultural differences and respect in own company and Cultural differences and respect in the other company table the correlation results are divided into three major rows: the first contains the Pearson r values, the second contains the probabilities of obtaining those values if the null hypothesis was true, and the third provides sample size.

The correlation matrix table includes the correlation, p-value, and number of observations for each pair of variables in the model. For unequal number of observations for each pair, SPSS removes cases from the regression analysis which do not have complete data on all variables selected for the model. It can be noticed the lack of multicollinearity. The two predictors are not strongly related (r = -.193, p = .116). This indicates adherence to one of the assumptions of regression.

The Model Summary for Integration outcome by Cultural differences and respect in own company and Cultural differences and respect in the other company table provides an overview of the results. Of primary interest are the R Square and Adjusted R Square values. It provides the Multiple Correlation (R = .304), the Multiple Correlation squared (R^2 = .093), the adjusted Multiple Correlation squared (adj.R^2 = .044), and the Standard

Error of the Estimate which can be used to determine how well a regression model fits the data.

The multiple correlation coefficient R can be considered to be one measure of the quality of the prediction of the dependent variable. A value of 0.304 indicates a medium level of prediction. The R2 value (also called the coefficient of determination) is the proportion of variance in the dependent variable that can be explained by the independent variables (technically, it is the proportion of variation accounted for by the regression model above and beyond the mean model). The value of 0.093 indicates that the independent variables explain 9.3% of the variability of the dependent variable.

The multiple correlation refers to the combined correlation of each predictor with the outcome. The multiple correlation squared represents the amount of variance in the outcome which is accounted for by the predictors; here, 9.3% of the variance in Integration outcome is accounted for by both Cultural differences and respect in own company and Cultural differences and respect in the other company. However, the multiple correlation squared is a bit optimistic, and therefore, the adjusted R^2 is more appropriate.

The ANOVA for Integration outcome by Cultural differences and respect in own company and Cultural differences and respect in the other company table shows the test of significance of the model using an ANOVA. There are 39 (N - 1) total degrees of freedom. With two predictors, the Regression effect has two degrees of freedom. The Regression effect is statistically significant indicating that prediction of the dependent variable is accomplished better than can be done by chance. The *F*-ratio in the ANOVA table tests whether the overall regression model is a good fit for the data. The table shows that the independent variables statistically significantly predict the dependent variable, $F\,(2, 37) = 1.890$, $p = 0.165$ (the regression model is a good fit of the data).

Table 44 presents the Coefficients for Integration outcome by Cultural differences and respect in own company and Cultural differences and respect in the other company. The first two columns contain unstandardized (or raw score) coefficients and their standard errors. Unstandardized coefficients indicate how much the dependent variable varies with an independent variable when all other independent variables are held constant. The Constant coefficient is simply the y-intercept term for a linear best fit fine representing our fitted model. The Cultural differences and respect in own company and Cultural differences and respect in the other company unstandardized coefficients represent the weight applied to each score (for each variable) to produce new Integration outcome scores along the best fit line. The unstandardized coefficients are used to build the linear regression equation one might use to predict new scores of Integration outcome using available scores of Cultural differences and respect in own company and Cultural differences and respect in own company. The equation is below:

(Integration outcome) = -.302 *
(Cultural differences and respect in own company) + -.120 *
(Cultural differences and respect in the other company) + 3.674 (38)

Table 44. Coefficients for integration outcome by cultural differences and respect in own company and cultural differences and respect in the other company

Model		Unstandardized Coefficients		Standardized Coefficients	t	Sig.
		B	Std. Error	Beta		
1	(Constant)	3.674	.154		23.803	.000
	Cultural differences and respect in own company	-.302	.159	-.304	-1.908	.064
	Cultural differences and respect in the other company	-.120	.163	-.118	-.737	.466

The Standardized Coefficients, which are typically reported in social science journals (rather than the unstandardized coefficients) as a way of interpreting variable importance because, they can be directly compared (they are in the same metric). The standardized coefficients use the symbol Beta, which is the capital Greek letter β and can be interpreted as the correlation between a predictor and the outcome variable. There is no constant or y-intercept term when referring to standardized scores because, the y-intercept when graphing them is always zero. The standardization transformation results in a mean of 0 and a standard deviation of 1 for all variables so transformed.

The *Y* intercept of the raw score model is labelled as the Constant and has a value of 3.674. Of primary interest here are the raw (B) and standardized (Beta) coefficients, and their significance levels determined by *t* tests. The predictors are statistically significant, except for Cultural differences and respect in the other company.

The calculated t-score for each unstandardized coefficient (coefficient divided by standard error) and their associated p-value are presented in the last two columns.

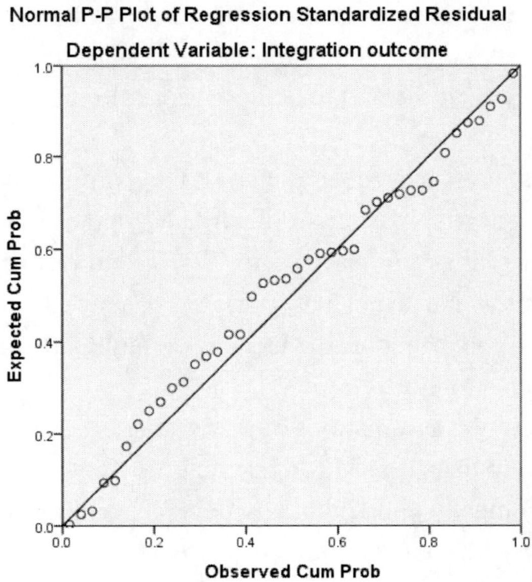

Figure 28. Normal P-P Plot of Regression Standardized Residual values for Integration outcome by Cultural differences and respect in own company and Cultural differences and respect in the other company.

Figure 28 presents the Normal P-P Plot of Regression Standardized Residual values for Integration outcome by Cultural differences and respect in own company and Cultural differences and respect in the other company.

It shows that the values are very close to the reference line, which indicates very little deviation of the expected values from the observed values.

8.13. M&A Outcome Dependence of Cultural Differences and Respect in Own Company and Cultural Differences and Respect in the Other Company

In the Correlations for M&A outcome by Cultural differences and respect in own company and Cultural differences and respect in the other company table the correlation results are divided into three major rows: the first contains the Pearson r values, the second contains the probabilities of obtaining those values if the null hypothesis was true, and the third provides sample size.

The correlation matrix table includes the correlation, p-value, and number of observations for each pair of variables in the model. For unequal number of observations for each pair, SPSS removes cases from the regression analysis which do not have complete data on all variables selected for the model. It can be noticed the lack of multicollinearity. The two predictors are not strongly related (r = -.193, p = .116). This indicates adherence to one of the assumptions of regression.

The Model Summary for M&A outcome by Cultural differences and respect in own company and Cultural differences and respect in the other company table provides an overview of the results. Of primary interest are the R Square and Adjusted R Square values. It provides the Multiple Correlation (R = .321), the Multiple Correlation squared (R^2 = .103), the adjusted Multiple Correlation squared (adj.R^2 = .054), and the Standard Error of the Estimate which can be used to determine how well a regression model fits the data.

The multiple correlation coefficient R can be considered to be one measure of the quality of the prediction of the dependent variable. A value of 0.321 indicates a medium level of prediction. The R2 value (also called the coefficient of determination) is the proportion of variance in the dependent variable that can be explained by the independent variables (technically, it is the proportion of variation accounted for by the regression model above and beyond the mean model). The value of 0.103 indicates that the independent variables explain 10.3% of the variability of the dependent variable.

The multiple correlation refers to the combined correlation of each predictor with the outcome. The multiple correlation squared represents the amount of variance in the outcome which is accounted for by the predictors; here, 10.3% of the variance in M&A outcome is accounted for by both Cultural differences and respect in own company and Cultural differences and respect in the other company. However, the multiple correlation squared is a bit optimistic, and therefore, the adjusted R^2 is more appropriate.

The ANOVA for M&A outcome by Cultural differences and respect in own company and Cultural differences and respect in the other company table shows the test of significance of the model using an ANOVA. There are 39 (N - 1) total degrees of freedom. With two predictors, the Regression effect has two degrees of freedom. The Regression effect is statistically significant indicating that prediction of the dependent variable is accomplished better than can be done by chance. The *F*-ratio in the **ANOVA** table tests whether the overall regression model is a good fit for the data. The table shows that the independent variables statistically significantly predict the dependent variable, F (2, 37) = 2.121, $p = 0.134$ (the regression model is a good fit of the data).

Table 45 presents the Coefficients for M&A outcome by Cultural differences and respect in own company and Cultural differences and respect in the other company. The first two columns contain unstandardized (or raw score) coefficients and their standard errors. Unstandardized coefficients indicate how much the dependent variable varies with an independent variable when all other independent variables are held constant. The Constant coefficient is simply the y-intercept term for a linear best fit fine representing our fitted model. The Cultural differences and respect in own company and Cultural differences and respect in the other company unstandardized coefficients represent the weight applied to each score (for each variable) to produce new M&A outcome scores along the best fit line. The unstandardized coefficients are used to build the linear regression equation one might use to predict new scores of M&A outcome using available scores of Cultural differences and respect in own company and Cultural differences and respect in own company. The equation is below:

(M&A outcome) = -.243 *
(Cultural differences and respect in own company) - .048 *
(Cultural differences and respect in the other company) + 3.822 (39)

The Standardized Coefficients, which are typically reported in social science journals (rather than the unstandardized coefficients) as a way of interpreting variable importance because, they can be directly compared (they are in the same metric). The standardized coefficients use the symbol Beta, which is the capital Greek letter β and can be interpreted as the correlation between a predictor and the outcome variable. There is no constant or y-intercept term when referring to standardized scores because, the y-intercept when graphing them is always zero. The standardization transformation results in a mean of 0 and a standard deviation of 1 for all variables so transformed.

Table 45. Coefficients for M&A outcome by cultural differences and respect in own company and cultural differences and respect in the other company

Model		Unstandardized Coefficients		Standardized Coefficients	t	Sig.
		B	Std. Error	Beta		
1	(Constant)	3.822	.115		33.229	.000
	Cultural differences and respect in own company	-.243	.118	-.327	-2.059	.047
	Cultural differences and respect in the other company	-.048	.121	-.063	-.398	.693

The *Y* intercept of the raw score model is labelled as the Constant and has a value of 3.822. Of primary interest here are the raw (B) and standardized (Beta) coefficients, and their significance levels determined by *t* tests. The predictors are statistically significant, except for Cultural differences and respect in the other company.

The calculated t-score for each unstandardized coefficient (coefficient divided by standard error) and their associated p-value are presented in the last two columns.

Figure 29 presents the Normal P-P Plot of Regression Standardized Residual values for M&A outcome by Cultural differences and respect in own company and Cultural differences and respect in the other company. It shows that the values are very close to the reference line, which indicates very little deviation of the expected values from the observed values.

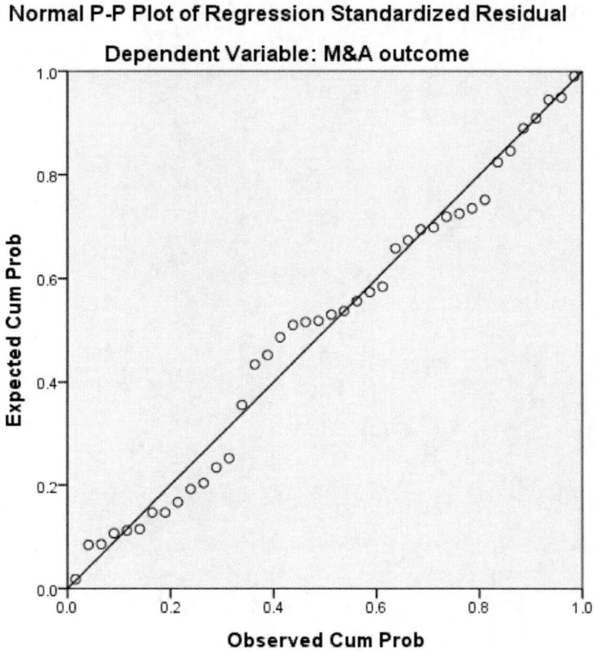

Figure 29. Normal P-P Plot of Regression Standardized Residual values for M&A outcome by Cultural differences and respect in own company and Cultural differences and respect in the other company.

Chapter 9

PERCEPTION ON THE M&A INTEGRATION PROCESS AND OUTCOME

The General Linear Model was applied.

A univariate GLM tests only one dependent variable. There can be one or more independent variables and/or factors. A one-way ANOVA is a univariate GLM with one independent variable. A two-way ANOVA is a univariate GLM with two independent variables.

Interactions between factors as well as the effects of individual factors can be investigated. Also, the effects of covariates and covariate interactions with factors can be included.

The first test performed is Levene's Test of Equality of Error Variance. The significance of Levene's test for equality of variance is used as the criteria for satisfying the assumption. SPSS computes the Levene test as part of the output for general linear models.

Table no. 46 presents the homogeneity test on the two groups of data (df = 2). For further processing will be selected only the data were "Sig." is at least 0.2 which is clearly not significant (marked in bold).

Table 46. Homogeneity test results (Levene's Test of Equality of Error Variances)

No.	Dependent Variable	Independent Variables	F	df1	df2	Sig.
1	**Intercultural competence**	**Culture Cluster and Total number of languages**	**1.261**	**18**	**29**	**.282**
2	Conflict prevention	Culture Cluster and Level of education	1.539	13	33	.155
3	National culture, importance for a cross border M&A	Culture Cluster and Number of foreign languages	1.411	17	32	.195
4	Organizational culture, importance for a cross border M&A	Culture Cluster and Job level	1.654	10	39	.128
5	Professional culture, importance for a cross border M&A	Culture Cluster and Profession	1.987	12	34	.058
6	Top management's actions, impact on M&A success	Culture Cluster and Profession	2.880	13	35	.006
7	National culture, impact on the success/failure of the M&A process	Culture Cluster and Total number of languages	1.510	18	29	.157
8	Organizational culture, impact on the success/failure of the M&A process	Culture Cluster and Level of education	2.371	13	34	.022
9	Professional culture, impact on the success/failure of the M&A process	Culture Cluster and Profession	1.651	13	34	.119
10	**Profit of my company change estimation**	**Culture Cluster and Profession**	**1.072**	**12**	**31**	**.415**
11	**Profit of the other company change estimation**	**Culture Cluster and Profession**	**1.309**	**11**	**29**	**.269**
12	**Sales of my company change estimation**	**Culture Cluster and Level of education**	**1.198**	**13**	**28**	**.331**
13	**Sales of the other company change estimation**	**Culture Cluster and Level of education**	**1.419**	**13**	**27**	**.214**
14	Market share of my company change estimation	Culture Cluster and Profession	1.943	11	30	.073
15	**Market share of the other company change estimation**	**Culture Cluster and Profession**	**1.415**	**11**	**28**	**.221**

No.	Dependent Variable	Independent Variables	F	df1	df2	Sig.
16	Return on equity (ROE) of my company change estimation	Culture Cluster and Level of education	2.509	13	25	.023
17	Return on equity (ROE) of the other company change estimation	Culture Cluster and Level of education	1.837	13	25	.093
18	Return on assets (ROA) of my company change estimation	Culture Cluster and Job level	2.127	10	28	.057
19	Return on assets (ROA) of the other company change estimation	Culture Cluster and Job level	3.486	10	26	.005

Table 47. Grand Mean results

No.	Dependent Variable	Independent Variables	Mean	Std. Error	95% Confidence Interval	
					Lower Bound	Upper Bound
1.	Intercultural competence	Culture Cluster and Total number of languages	-.163[a]	.201	-.574	.247
2.	Profit of my company change estimation	Culture Cluster and Profession	3.338[a]	.176	2.980	3.696
3.	Profit of the other company change estimation	Culture Cluster and Profession	3.890[a]	.190	3.501	4.278
4.	Sales of my company change estimation	Culture Cluster and Level of education	3.565[a]	.179	3.200	3.931
5.	Sales of the other company change estimation	Culture Cluster and Level of education	3.810[a]	.148	3.505	4.114
6.	Market share of the other company change estimation	Culture Cluster and Profession	3.593[a]	.179	3.226	3.960

The Bonferroni multiple comparisons will be tested where the equal variances assumption is satisfied. Post hoc tests may be carried out in response to the obtained data. The Bonferroni test is a set of t-tests of the difference for all possible pairs with an adjusted alpha for each t-test so that the total alpha for all comparisons does not exceed the desired level of significance. The post hoc tests indicate the differences in model-predicted means for pairs of factor levels.

The estimated marginal means and profile plots might uncover an interaction between the factors, that is shown in the profile plots.

Table 47 presents the model-estimated marginal means and standard errors of the dependent variables at the factor combinations of independent variables. The table is helpful for exploring the interaction effect between the factors.

9.1. Intercultural Competence Dependence of Culture Cluster and Total Number of Languages

The post hoc test shows a difference in the impact of the Intercultural competence between different Total number of languages.

In the Profile Plot for Intercultural competence can be noticed that the difference in Intercultural competence between different Culture Clusters is greater for smaller Total number of languages.

The estimated marginal means and profile plots uncovered an interaction between the two factors. The strong interaction effect is improbable to be due to chance.

9.2. Profit of My Company Change Estimation Dependence of Culture Cluster and Profession

In the Profile Plot for Profit of my company change estimation can be noticed that the difference in Profit of my company change estimation between different Culture Clusters is greater for Economists and Others than for Engineers.

The estimated marginal means and profile plots uncovered an interaction between the two factors. The strong interaction effect is improbable to be due to chance.

9.3. Profit of the Other Company Change Estimation Dependence of Culture Cluster and Profession

In the Profile Plot for Profit of the other company change estimation can be noticed that the difference in Profit of the other company change estimation between different Culture Clusters is greater for Economists than for Engineers and Others.

The estimated marginal means and profile plots uncovered an interaction between the two factors. The strong interaction effect is improbable to be due to chance.

9.4. Sales of My Company Change Estimation Dependence of Culture Cluster and Level of Education

The post hoc test shows a difference in the Sales of my company change estimation between Graduate, Master degree, PhD and Post graduate education.

In the Profile Plot for Sales of my company change estimation can be noticed that. the difference in Sales of my company change estimation between different Culture Clusters is greater for Graduate than for Master degree and PhD.

The estimated marginal means and profile plots uncovered an interaction between the two factors. The strong interaction effect is improbable to be due to chance.

9.5. Sales of the Other Company Change Estimation Dependence of Culture Cluster and Level of Education

The post hoc test shows a difference in the Sales of the other company change estimation between Graduate, Master degree, PhD and Post graduate education.

In the Profile Plot for Sales of the other company change estimation can be noticed that the difference in Sales of the other company change estimation between different Culture Clusters is greater for Graduate than for Master degree and PhD.

The estimated marginal means and profile plots uncovered an interaction between the two factors. The strong interaction effect is improbable to be due to chance.

9.6. Market Share of the Other Company Change Estimation Dependence of Culture Cluster and Profession

In the Profile Plot for Market share of the other company change estimation can be noticed that the difference in Market share of the other company change estimation between different Culture Clusters is greater for Economists than for Engineers and Others.

The estimated marginal means and profile plots uncovered an interaction between the two factors. The strong interaction effect is improbable to be due to chance.

Chapter 10

CONCLUSION

This chapter presents a brief overview of the most significant facets of this book, a discussion of the findings and their implications and a depiction of the conclusions of the study.

This book is focused on post-investment issues, particularly on intercultural synergy, and M&A performance.

The most challenging part of the M&A process is the integration of two entities that present different organizational and national cultures. The contradictory findings in the existing studies impose further empirical research on the relationship between culture, post-merger integration processes, and M&A performance.

In lieu of asking if cultural differences have an impact on performance, researchers should concentrate on how cultural differences affect M&A performance.

Post-merger integration phase is a complex operation of mixing and repositioning processes to reify synergies that typically stimulate mergers and acquisitions.

Intercultural synergy is the mixture of diverse cultural elements like traditions, values, norms, practices, behaviors etc. in such a way that the result is a construction of higher value than the sum of elements.

This book exerts to find an explanation for M&A performance in terms of the impact that cultural differences have on the post-merger integration process. It emphasises the role of post-investment monitoring and intercultural synergies achievement.

The M&A reasons are the result of globalisation, of the need of growth and of achieving synergies. Most of the professionals consider that M&A is one of the most significant business phenomena in the past decades and it will remain in the future too. At the same time scholars and practitioners warn about the M&A dangers.

Generically, M&A researchers have concentrated independently on pre-acquisition and post-acquisition influential factors. They do not have an extensive insight of the M&A process. Thus, M&As are a complex domain demanding an interdisciplinary approach. Whereas M&A has been granted more research attention in the last decades, this domain is still a practical challenge.

Mergers and acquisitions (M&As) have been studied by many scholars. Each group explored the topic from a unique perspective. This study uncovered various interpretations of intercultural particularities. Therefore, it can be observed that the almost general opinion is that cultural influences are important in M&A. Despite this, the outcomes of this study reveal the underestimation of the role of cultural integration in M&A literature.

This study is seeking to deepen the apprehension of the impact of cultural differences on M&A performance. Regardless of the increased attention directed at the implications of cultural differences for the M&A performance the outcomes are still doubtful. Some scholars think that cultural differences might affect the M&A process while others assert a positive effect in M&A performance based on synergy creation. Still, most of the scholars and practitioners point to the significant influence of intercultural aspects on M&A performance. Summarizing the contradictory findings, cultural differences in organizations can be both an asset and a liability and the intercultural issues require more theoretical and empirical study.

Many scholars have stated that is difficult to analyse post-merger integration although the integration phase is critical due to the significant cultural differences of the two different organisations. There are irresolute evidences on how integration is accomplished. The influence of cultural differences is sometimes antithetical.

The integration process is critical in cross-border M&A but it is difficult to analyze post-merger integration due to the different manners of interpreting and reconstructing the integration process. Culture is habitually considered an obstacle to the success of M&As. Notwithstanding other authors posit that cultural distance can enhance the performance of cross-border acquisitions by providing access to the partner's routines and repertoires embedded in national culture.

The concept of "intercultural synergy" is still poorly understood despite a growing body of research on synergy creation. Generically, there is an inadequate practical approach although most scholars highlight the importance of intercultural synergy in M&A.

Unquestionably, there is a need to amplify the studies on intercultural synergy.

M&A performance can be characterized by ambiguity of the concept and a lack of concurrence on measurement procedures. The majority of the professionals consider that the misunderstanding of the nature and sources of the intercultural synergy is a cause for M&As underperformance.

Cultural synergy can be produced by similarities in organisations but at once by differences. Empirical studies deliver contradictory results. Intercultural synergy might be highly significant after the merger or on the contrary have an insignificant effect on firms' performance or even a negative impact. The findings regarding the cross-cultural integration aspects are contradictory and the relation between M&A performance and intercultural synergy is still unclear.

To sum up, these findings suggest that intercultural synergy is a significant and controversial issue of cross border M&As. The inconsistent results suggest the need for further research on post-merger integration.

The main goal of this study was to uncover intercultural issues that managers encountered during the post-investment phase and they should have discovered during the pre-investment phase. Intercultural synergy has a strong impact on M&A. Both national and organizational cultures are determinants for maximizing the intercultural synergy.

A quantitative descriptive approach was employed in this study. In order to examine managers' perceptual evaluations of cultural differences and merger/acquisition outcomes it was used a questionnaire. The data collection process was in absence of an interviewer and was done remotely, mainly by e-mail. Well-defined research questions were used and newly generated numerical data were obtained by converting the levels of perception using the Likert scale. The cross-sectional survey design was considered the most appropriate for this study. It was used snowball sampling. Managers from different countries who experienced first-hand the M&As and post-investment intercultural integration processes are the target of this study. The target of the survey was cross-border M&A. Respondents were asked to indicate the level of cultural differences between the companies before and after the M&A.

The specific questions of this study are: (1) Do the cultural differences lead to synergy effects?; (2) Do the cultural differences influence M&A's outcomes?; (3) Does the cultural specificity affect the perception on the M&A integration process and outcome?

The independent variables for the first two research questions are the national/organizational cultural characteristics. The independent variables for the third research question are attributes of the respondents.

The dependent variables are managers' M&A integration and outcome satisfaction in general and within particular facets and the perception on cultural differences. Respondents were asked to indicate the level of cultural differences between the companies before and after the M&A. The dependent variables are aggregation of individual attributes.

Data Analysis begins with an analysis on the profile of the respondents and the background of their companies. Based on Factor Analysis, a number of 19 factors were extracted structured in 9 groups (dimensions). They all start from 77 basic items.

The nine dimensions obtained from the analysis are: Cultural differences between the companies before the merger/acquisition, Culture of own company before the merger/acquisition, Culture of the other company before the merger/acquisition, Cultural differences between the companies in the post-investment stage, Synergistic effects achieved by the integration of different areas, Organizational problems in own company as result of the merger/acquisition, Organizational problems in the other company as result of the merger/acquisition, Problems in cooperation between the two teams of top managers and Skills/abilities useful in the post-investment stage.

The 19 equations used to estimate the factors in relation to the items value offer a significant practical tool.

It can be highlighted the group related to synergy: Synergistic effects achieved by the integration of different areas. This group is based on Organizational functions (factor) and is a result of four basic items: Management, Finance, Production and Human resource management.

Among other groups related to organizational culture there are two groups concerning individuals and national culture: Problems in cooperation between the two teams of top managers and Skills/abilities useful in the post-investment stage. They correspond to Conflict prevention and Intercultural competence. The corresponding items are: Misunderstandings, Mistrust, Incapacity to reconcile different points of view, Unwillingness to reconcile different points of view, Conflicts, Cultural differences understanding, Multilingualism, Adaptation to a different culture, Awareness of own culture, Respect for otherness, Communicative awareness, Behavioral flexibility and Readiness for change. These are a significant practical tool.

Concerning the general issues in the post M&A stage the most important groups are: Organizational problems in own company as result of the merger/acquisition and Organizational problems in the other company as result of the merger/acquisition. They are the result of the following factors: Future insecurity, Organizational reliability, Organizational distrust and Resistance barriers.

General linear model was used in some of the cases because the analyses include both numeric (interval level) and categorical variables (nominal level). The other dependencies were studied using statistical regression.

The focal point of this study was to check whether there is a significant relationship between the M&A outcomes, synergy and the cultural differences. It examined also the relationship between the perception on the M&A integration process and outcome and the cultural specificity.

The use of regression and General Linear Model analyses assisted the statistical aims of the research by pointing out a positive considerable relationship.

Generally, the analysis results indicated a considerable relationship between the M&A outcomes, synergy and the cultural differences. The same can be said about the relationship between the perception on the M&A integration process and outcome and the cultural specificity.

It can be highlighted that the following two dependencies regarding New culture and New practices were satisfactorily confirmed: New culture by Cultural differences and respect in own company and Cultural differences and respect in the other company and New practices and Group identification in own company and Group identification in the other company.

The following dependency regarding synergy was also confirmed: Intercultural synergy based decisions by Cultural differences and respect in own company and Cultural differences and respect in the other company.

It deserves to be noticed the difference between Integration outcome and M&A outcome as ensues from the following dependencies: Integration outcome by Cultural differences and respect in own company and Cultural differences and respect in the other company and M&A outcome by Cultural differences and respect in own company and Cultural differences and respect in the other company

To summarize, the findings of this book might offer support for the interaction between cultural specificity and the post-M&A stage, as the cultural variables impact the perceptions on M&A outcomes, M&A integration and intercultural synergy creation, however modest the results are. This study expands the current paradigm of post-M&A activities to include the study of cultural issues by grouping them in factors and dimension. This is a significant implication, because most of perception and evaluation instruments are conceived for national culture or for organizational culture separately. The main theories, moreover, have also been almost exclusively developed not by taking into consideration the concept of intercultural synergy, as it is in the current study.

And yet, professionals world-wide face with the assignement of comprehending and examining M&A cultural issues across professional diversity.

Additionally, this study contributes to the intercultural management in M&A by integrating research on national, organizational and professional culture, into a theory of M&A performance and outcome. Also, this study strived to investigate not only the outcomes and intercultural synergy but the perception on these issues. In the past, the discussions focused mostly on post-M&A integration and outcomes and neglecting the impact of intercultural synergy. Moreover, studies dealing with post-M&A integration and monitoring were barely sufficient. The findings from this study reveal that to comprehend M&A performance it might be useful to examine the nature of culture-related synergetic processes, as they impact post-M&A integration.

A better understanding of the cultural differences before and after the M&A can help organizations and provide better opportunities for integration in cross border M&A. With the increase of global mobility, intercultural synergy becomes increasingly signifcant. Multi-national organizations might gather a competitive advantage when they understand the importance of cultural synergy.

In the area of intercultural management, the findings from this study reveal that the Culture Clusters is a very helpful and strong tool that requires further investigation. It appears that national culture might influence perceptions on M&A in some culture clusters much more than in others. These findings suggest that there is a need to further examine the mechanism employed in the process of integration and synergy creation across cultures and how post investment monitoring impacts the M&A performance.

Lastly, M&A scholars and practitioners may profit from a better comprehension of cultural values that impact the perceptions of individuals during post M&A integration stage across cultures. Global companies that minimize the importance and the right content of post M&A monitoring assume higher risk of failure.

Confidently that these outcomes would forewarn other M&A professionals of the necessity to deeply understand the cultural issues influencing the post-M&A processes, the author will continue the research especially in the intercultural synergy domain.

Based on the outcomes of this study which suggest a mixed effect of national, organizational and professional cultures, future research may consider the dynamic nature of a wider spectrum of cultural influences on post-M&A stage perceptions. Such investigation would conduct to a better understanding of the intercultural synergy in M&A and how organizations can benefit from such an opportunity.

In the area of intercultural management, the findings from this book indicate that the Culture Clusters is a very useful and powerful tool and it deserves further investigation.

Lastly, future studies should consider a better definition of the "intercultural synergy" concept itself. The concept of "intercultural synergy" is still poorly understood despite a growing body of research on synergy creation. Moreover, post-merger integration needs a unification of the different manners of interpreting and reconstructing the process. Additionally, it would be useful to further examine the mechanism employed in the process of integration and synergy creation across cultures and how post investment monitoring impacts the M&A performance.

APPENDIX: QUESTIONNAIRE

Dear Respondent,

I would like to invite you to participate in a research study entitled: Post-investment monitoring. Intercultural synergy valuation.

This study attempts to explain M&A outcomes in terms of the impact of cultural differences on the post-M&A integration process. The findings are intended to support practitioners in their future M&A activity. To fill out the survey should not take more than 20-25 minutes.

The survey is confidential. Survey results will be presented as summary information only, and no individual answers will be shared.

Thank you very much for taking the time to participate in this survey,

Sincerely,
Liviu Warter

M&A EXPERIENCE

Looking at your most recent or most important merger or acquisition, please respond the questions to follow.

1. In how many mergers or acquisitions has your company participated during the 10 years before this merger/acquisition?

   0 1-3 4-6 7-9 more than 10

2. In how many mergers or acquisitions have you participated during the 10 years before this merger/acquisition?

   0 1-3 4-6 7-9 more than 10

3. What is the size of the merger/acquisition (million EUR)?

   0-3 4-10 11-20 21-50 more than 50

4. Did you work with the acquired company, the acquirer or it was a merger?

   Acquired Acquirer Merger

CULTURAL DIFFERENCES (INTERCULTURAL SYNERGY)

5. How would you describe the cultural differences between the companies before the merger/acquisition in the following areas?

	No differences		Significant differences		
Management	1	2	3	4	5
Company values and practices	1	2	3	4	5
Finance	1	2	3	4	5
Production	1	2	3	4	5
Human resource management	1	2	3	4	5

6. How would you describe the cultural differences between the companies in the post-investment stage in the following areas?

	No differences				Significant differences
Management	1	2	3	4	5
Company values and practices	1	2	3	4	5
Finance	1	2	3	4	5
Production	1	2	3	4	5
Human resource management	1	2	3	4	5

7. How would you describe the culture of your company before the merger/acquisition?

Contains many different cultural groups 1 2 3 4 5
Contains few different cultural groups

High level of valuing cultural differences 1 2 3 4 5
Low level of valuing cultural differences

High tolerance of cultural differences 1 2 3 4 5
Low tolerance of cultural differences

Multiculturalism 1 2 3 4 5
Uniculturalism

Weak belief in own competitiveness 1 2 3 4 5
Very strong belief in own competitiveness

Weak identity 1 2 3 4 5
Strong identity

No sense of belonging together 1 2 3 4 5
Strong sense of belonging together

Great readiness for change 1 2 3 4 5 No readiness for change

High level of flexibility 1 2 3 4 5 Low level of flexibility

High level of creativity 1 2 3 4 5 Low level of creativity

8. How would you describe the culture of the other company before the merger/acquisition?

Contains many different cultural groups 1 2 3 4 5 Contains few different cultural groups

High level of valuing cultural differences 1 2 3 4 5 Low level of valuing cultural differences

High tolerance of cultural differences 1 2 3 4 5 Low tolerance of cultural differences

Multiculturalism 1 2 3 4 5 Uniculturalism

Weak belief in own competitiveness 1 2 3 4 5 Very strong belief in own competitiveness

Weak identity 1 2 3 4 5 Strong identity

No sense of belonging together 1 2 3 4 5 Strong sense of belonging together

Great readiness for change	1 2 3 4 5	No readiness for change
High level of flexibility	1 2 3 4 5	Low level of flexibility
High level of creativity	1 2 3 4 5	Low level of creativity

9. To what extent has the top management of the companies wanted to preserve its own culture?

	Not at all		Very much		
My company	1	2	3	4	5
The other company	1	2	3	4	5

10. How did the top management of the companies view the practices and values of the other company?

	Very negative		Very positive		
My company	1	2	3	4	5
The other company	1	2	3	4	5

11. To what extent have the practices and values of the companies dominated in the integration process?

	Not at all		Very much		
My company	1	2	3	4	5
The other company	1	2	3	4	5

12. To what extent has a new culture shared by the two teams of top managers been created after the merger/acquisition?

Not at all		Very much		
1	2	3	4	5

13. To what extent have new practices shared by the two teams of top managers been created after the merger/acquisition?

Not at all		Very much		
1	2	3	4	5

14. To what extent have the decisions been based on maximization of intercultural synergy?

Not at all			Very much	
1	2	3	4	5

15. In your opinion, is culture important for a cross border M&A?

	Not at all		Very much		
National culture	1	2	3	4	5
Organizational culture	1	2	3	4	5
Professional culture	1	2	3	4	5

16. In your opinion, which ones of the following skills or abilities have been useful in the post-investment stage?

	Not at all		Very useful		
Cultural differences understanding	1	2	3	4	5
Multilingualism	1	2	3	4	5
Adaptation to a different culture	1	2	3	4	5
Awareness of own culture	1	2	3	4	5
Respect for otherness	1	2	3	4	5
Communicative awareness	1	2	3	4	5

Behavioral flexibility	1	2	3	4	5
Readiness for change	1	2	3	4	5

17. How did the top management of the companies view the merger/acquisition?

	Very negative		Very positive		
My company	1	2	3	4	5
The other company	1	2	3	4	5

OUTCOME OF THE MERGER/ACQUISITION

18. As a result of the merger/acquisition, have there been following organizational problems in your company?

	Not at all		Very much		
Uncertainty about the future	1	2	3	4	5
Divergent goals and objectives	1	2	3	4	5
Poor coordination/integration	1	2	3	4	5
Low professional trust	1	2	3	4	5
Mistrust in rewards system	1	2	3	4	5
Mistrust in advancement opportunities	1	2	3	4	5
Poor communication	1	2	3	4	5
Loss of key persons	1	2	3	4	5
Lack of motivation	1	2	3	4	5
Poor integration leadership	1	2	3	4	5
Low organizational identification	1	2	3	4	5
Low intercultural synergy	1	2	3	4	5
Increase in absenteeism	1	2	3	4	5
Resistance to change	1	2	3	4	5
Sabotage	1	2	3	4	5

19. As a result of the merger/acquisition, have there been following organizational problems in the other company?

	Not at all		Very much		
Uncertainty about the future	1	2	3	4	5
Divergent goals and objectives	1	2	3	4	5
Poor coordination/integration	1	2	3	4	5
Low professional trust	1	2	3	4	5
Mistrust in rewards system	1	2	3	4	5
Mistrust in advancement opportunities	1	2	3	4	5
Poor communication	1	2	3	4	5
Loss of key persons	1	2	3	4	5
Lack of motivation	1	2	3	4	5
Poor integration leadership	1	2	3	4	5
Low organizational identification	1	2	3	4	5
Low intercultural synergy	1	2	3	4	5
Increase in absenteeism	1	2	3	4	5
Resistance to change	1	2	3	4	5
Sabotage	1	2	3	4	5

20. In your opinion, have there been problems in cooperation between the two teams of top managers?

	Not at all		Very much		
Misunderstandings	1	2	3	4	5
Mistrust	1	2	3	4	5
Incapacity to reconcile different points of view	1	2	3	4	5
Unwillingness to reconcile different points of view	1	2	3	4	5
Conflicts	1	2	3	4	5

21. As a result of the merger/acquisition, estimate the extent to which you agree with the following statements:

Almost all top managers of my company have remained in the company after the merger/acquisition

Do not agree			Completely agree	
1	2	3	4	5

Almost all top managers of the other company have remained in the company after the merger/acquisition

Do not agree			Completely agree	
1	2	3	4	5

22. When evaluating the post-investment stage, have synergistic effects been achieved by the integration of different areas?

	Not at all		Very much		
Management	1	2	3	4	5
Finance	1	2	3	4	5
Production	1	2	3	4	5
Human resource management	1	2	3	4	5

23. In your opinion, how much has the top managers' degree of autonomy affected the outcome of the merger/acquisition?

Not at all			Very much	
1	2	3	4	5

24. How much has the possible organizational change resistance affected the top management's decisions?

Not at all			Very much	
1	2	3	4	5

25. In your opinion, how much have the top management's decisions affected the outcome of the integration process?

Not at all			Very much	
1	2	3	4	5

26. How much does the success of a merger/acquisition depend on the top management's actions, according to your opinion?

Not at all			Very much	
1	2	3	4	5

27. Have there been conflicts between the top managers of the two companies?

	Not at all		Very much		
Open conflicts	1	2	3	4	5
Covered/hidden conflicts	1	2	3	4	5

28. In your opinion, how has the integration of the companies succeeded?

Total failure			Great success	
1	2	3	4	5

29. What is the outcome of the merger/acquisition, according to your opinion?

Total failure			Great success	
1	2	3	4	5

30. In your opinion, how have cultural differences affected the success/failure of the merger/acquisition?

	Not at all		Very much		
National culture	1	2	3	4	5
Organizational culture	1	2	3	4	5
Professional culture	1	2	3	4	5

31. Please estimate the change of the following indicators after the merger/acquisition:

	Significantly weakened		Significantly improved		
Profit of my company	1	2	3	4	5
Profit of the other company	1	2	3	4	5
Sales of my company	1	2	3	4	5
Sales of the other company	1	2	3	4	5
Market share of my company	1	2	3	4	5
Market share of the other company	1	2	3	4	5
Return on equity (ROE) of my company	1	2	3	4	5
Return on equity (ROE) of the other company	1	2	3	4	5
Return on assets (ROA) of my company	1	2	3	4	5
Return on assets (ROA) of the other company	1	2	3	4	5

32. How clear was this questionnaire?

Not at all		Very much		
1	2	3	4	5

BACKGROUND OF THE RESPONDENT

Please, provide the following information about you:

- Native language(s):--
- Country of origin:---
- Gender: --
- Profession:--
- Level of education:---
- Job level :--
- Foreign language(s):--
- Company name:--

REFERENCES

Ahammad, M. F., Glaister, K. W., Weber, Y., & Tarba, S. Y. (2012). Top management retention in cross-border acquisitions: the roles of financial incentives, acquirer's commitment and autonomy. *European J. International Management*, 6(4), 458–480.

Ahammad, M. F., et al.(2014).Knowledge transfer and cross-border acquisition performance: The impact of cultural distance and employee retention. *International Business Review*, http://dx.doi. org/10.1016/ j.ibusrev.2014.06.015.

Ahammad, F., Tarba, S.Y., Liu, Y., & Glaister, K. W. (2016). Knowledge transfer and cross-border acquisition performance: The impact of cultural distance and employee retention. *International Business Review*, 25, 66–75.

Almor, T., Tarba, S. Y., & Margalit, A. (2014). Maturing, Technology-Based, Born-Global Companies: Surviving Through Mergers and Acquisitions. *Management International Review*, 54, 421-444.

Angwin, D. N., Meadows, M. (2014). New Integration Strategies for Post-Acquisition Management. *Long Range Planning*, http://dx.doi. org/10.1016/j.lrp.2014.04.001.

Arikawa, Y., & Takechi, K. (2012). *In Search of Synergy Effects: Mergers and Productivity*. Retrieved from http://ssrn.com/abstract= 2156735.

Arvanitis, S., & Stucki, T. (2014). How Swiss small and medium-sized firms assess the performance impact of mergers and acquisitions. *Small Bus Econ*, 42, 339-360.

Arvanitis, S., Lokshin, B., Mohnen, P., & Woerter, M. (2015). Impact of External Knowledge Acquisition Strategies on Innovation A Comparative Study Based on Dutch and Swiss Panel Data. *Rev Ind Organ*, 46, 359–382.

Arvey, R., Dhanaraj. C., Javidan, M., & Zhang, Z. X. (2015). Are there unique leadership models in Asia? Exploring uncharted territory. *The Leadership Quarterly*, 26,1-6.

Babatunde, Y., & Low, S. P. (2015). *Cross-Cultural Management and Quality Performance Chinese Construction Firms in Nigeria*. Singapore: Springer Science+Business Media.

Baker McKenzie. (2018). *Global Transactions Forecast 2019 Dealing with the Uncertainty*. Retrieved from https://www.bakermckenzie.com/en/insight/publications/2018/12/global-transactions-forecast-2019.

Barmeyer, C. & Mayrhofer U. (2008). The contribution of intercultural management to the success of international mergers and acquisitions: An analysis of the EADS group. *International Business Review*, 17, 28-38.

Basuil, D. A. & Datta, D. K. (2015). Effects of Industry- and Region-Specific Acquisition Experience on Value Creation in Cross-Border Acquisitions: The Moderating Role of Cultural Similarity. *Journal of Management Studies,* 52(6), doi: 10.1111/joms.12128.

Bauer, F. & Matzler, K. (2014). Antecedents of M&A Success: The Role of Strategic Complementarity, Cultural Fit, and Degree and Speed of Integration. *Strategic Management Journal*, 35, 269-291.

Bauer, F., Hautz, J., & Matzler, K. (2015). Unveiling the myths of M&A integration: challenging general management and consulting practice. *Journal of Business Strategy*, 36(2), 16 – 24.

Bauer, F., Matzler, K., & Wolf, S. (2016). M&A and innovation: The role of integration and cultural differences—A central European targets perspective. *International Business Review*, 25, 76–86.

Bauer, F., Schriber, S., Degischer, D., & King, D. R. (2018). Contextualizing speed and cross-border acquisition performance: Labor market flexibility and efficiency effects. *Journal of World Business, 53*(2), 290-301. doi:10.1016/j.jwb.2018.01.001.

Bebenroth, R. (2015). *International Business Mergers and Acquisitions in Japan*. Japan: Springer.

Bertrand, O. & Capron, L. (2015). Productivity Enhancement at Home via Cross-Border Acquisitions: The Roles of Learning and Contemporaneous Domestic Investments. *Strategic Management Journal,* 36, 640–658.

Bingham, C. B., Heimeriks, K. H., Schijven, M., & Gates, S. (2014). Concurrent Learning How Firms Develop Multiple Dynamic Capabilities in Parallel. *Strategic Management Journal,* DOI: 10.1002/smj.2347.

Bird, A. & Mendenhall, M. E. (2016). From cross-cultural management to global leadership: Evolution and adaptation. *Journal of World Business*, 51, 115–126.

Björkman, I. & Welch, D. (2015). Framing the field of international human resource management research. *The International Journal of Human Resource Management*, 26(2), 136-150.

Blackard, K. & Gibson, G. W. (2002). Capitalizing On Conflict Strategies and Practices for Turning Conflict to Synergy. In *Organizations A Manager's Handbook*. California, Palo Alto: Davies-Black Publishing.

Bodner, J., & Capron, L. (2018). Post-merger integration. *Journal of Organization Design*, 7(3), 1-20. doi: 10.1186/s41469-018-0027-4.

Bond, M. H. (2014). How I am Constructing Culture-inclusive Theories of Social-psychological Process in our Age of Globalization. *Journal for the Theory of Social Behaviour,* 45(1). DOI: 10.1111/jtsb.12053

Brogiato, L. (2012). *Cross-cultural management integration in M&A M&As from China and India to mature markets in two key sectors: automotive and pharmaceutical. Intercultural issues and integration strategies*, Universita Ca' Foscari. Retrieved from http://dspace.unive.it/bitstream/handle/10579/1554/815916-1163367.pdf?sequence=2.

Brown, T. A. (2015). *Confirmatory Factor Analysis for Applied Research*, Second Edition. US: The Guilford Press.

Bureau Van Dijk. (2017). *Global M&A volume and value decline in 2016*. Retrieved from https://www.bvdinfo.com/getattachment/2f4eed2f-179b-43ce-b406-d187b93eee10/Global-M-A-volume-and-value-decline-in-2016.aspx.

Bureau Van Dijk. (2018). *Global M&A Review 2017*. Retrieved from https://www.bvdinfo.com/getattachment/0d5502bf-b54d-4f98-b100-4b1b4d3033cd/M-A-Review-Global-2017.aspx.

Bureau Van Dijk. (2019). *Global M&A Review 2018*. Retrieved from https://www.bvdinfo.com/BvD/media/reports/Global-M-AReview-2018.pdf.

Burghardt, D. & Helm, M. (2015). Firm growth in the course of mergers and acquisitions'. *Small Bus Econ*, 44, 889–904. DOI 10.1007/s11187-014-9624-y.

Calipha, R., Tarba, S., & Brock, D. (2012). Mergers and Acquisitions: A Review of Phases, Motives, and Success Factors. *Advances in Mergers and Acquisitions*, 9, 1-24.

Calipha, R., Brock, D. M., Rosenfeld, A., & Dvir, D. (2018). Acquired, transferred and integrated knowledge: A study of M&A knowledge performance. *Journal of Strategy and Management, 11*(3), 282-305. doi:10.1108/jsma-07-2017-0049.

Campbell, A. & Goold, M. (1998). *Synergy Why links between business units so often fail and how to make them work*. Oxford, UK: Capstone Publishing Limited.

Cartwright, S., Teerikangas, S., Rouzies, A., & Wilson-Evered, E. (2012). Methods in M&A–A look at the past and the future to forge a path forward. *Scandinavian Journal of Management*, 28, 95-106.

Center for Chemical Process Safety (CCPS) (2010). *Guidelines for Process Safety Acquisition Evaluation and Post Merger Integration*. New Jersey, Hoboken: John Wiley & Sons.

Chatterjee, S. (1986). Types of Synergy and Economic Value: The Impact of Acquisitions on Merging and Rival Firms. *Strategic Management Journal*, 7, 119-139.

Chatterjee, S. (1992). Sources of Value in Takeovers: Synergy or Restructuring-Implications for Target and Bidder Firms. *Strategic Management Journal*, 13, 267-286.

Chatterjee, S. (2007). Why is synergy so difficult in mergers of related businesses? *Strategy & Leadership,* 35(2), 46-52.

Chatterjee, S. (2009). The Keys to Successful Acquisition Programmes. *Long Range Planning*, 42, 137-163.

Chatterjee, S. & Brueller,N. N. (2015). A new M & A methodology: five lessons in anticipating post-merger resource interactions and challenges. *Strategy & Leadership*, 43(4), 26 – 37.

Cho, Y. S. & La, K. A. (2014). The Impact of Organizational Citizenship Behavior on Synergy Creation in Mergers and Acquisitions, According To Levels of Ocb and Types of M&A. *Academy of Accounting and Financial Studies Journal*, 18(2), 93–106.

Cicon, J., Clarke, J., Ferris, S. P., & Jayaraman, N. (2014). Managerial Expectations of Synergy and the Performance of Acquiring Firms: The Contribution of Soft Data. *Journal of Behavioral Finance*, 15(3), 161-175.

Clougherty, J. A. & Duso, T. (2011). Using rival effects to identify synergies and improve merger typologies. *Strategic Organization*, 9(4), 310-335.

CMS Legal Services (n.d.). *Emerging Europe: M&A Report 2014/15*. Retrieved from http://www.cmslegal.com/Hubbard.FileSystem/files/Publication/8808d40f-3708-4d33-af2f-993fe589ac39/Presentation/PublicationAttachment/bd5a78dc-b21b-4efd-98d3000d4f772e6e/FINAL%20Emerging%20Europe%20MA%20Deals%20report%202014%202015%20B.pdf.

Colman, H.L. & Grøgaard, B. (2013). Integration Vacuum: Creating Action Space for Global Strategy Implementation in International Acquisitions. *Thunderbird International Business Review*, 55(4), 405-418.

Dashti, Y. & Schwartz, D. (2015). The role and contribution of networks in M&A of innovative ventures: can lessons learned from networks of Israeli startups be applied by China? *Technology Analysis & Strategic Management*, 27(6), 628-645, DOI:10.1080/09537325. 2015.1018676.

David R. K. (n.d.). The Influence of Complementary Resources on Firm Boundary Decisions. [Electronic version] *Advances in Mergers and Acquisitions*, 25-42.

Deloitte (n.d).The Deloitte M&A Index 2016: *Opportunities amidst divergence*. Retrieved from http://www2.deloitte.com/uk/en/pages/financial-advisory/articles/deloitte-m-and-a-index.html.

Desai, J., Joshi, N. A., & Joshi, M. (n.d). *Upping the likelihood of Merger & Acquisition Success through Intercultural Synergy*. Retrieved from http://ssrn.com/abstract=1918708.

DePamphilis, D. (2012). *Mergers, Acquisitions, and Other Restructuring Activities: An Integrated Approach to Process, Tools, Cases, and Solutions.* Burlington, MA: Academic Press, Elsevier.

DePamphilis, D. (2011). *Mergers and Acquisitions Basics-Negotiation and Deal Structuring*. Burlington, MA: Academic Press, Elsevier.

DePamphilis, D. (2014). *Mergers, Acquisitions, and Other Restructuring Activities: An Integrated Approach to Process, Tools, Cases, and Solutions*. Burlington, MA: Academic Press, Elsevier.

De Bernardis, L. & Giustiniano, L. (2015). Evolution of multiple organisational identities after an M&A event. *Journal of Organizational Change Management*, 28(3), 333 – 355.

Dezi, L., Battisti, E., Ferraris, A., & Papa, A. (2018). The link between mergers and acquisitions and innovation. *Management Research Review*, 41(6), 716-752. doi:10.1108/mrr-07-2017-0213.

Doring, A. K., Schwartz, S. H. Cieciuch, J., Groenen, P. J. F. , Glatzel, V., Harasimczuk, J., Janowicz, N., Nyagolova, M., Scheefer, E. R., Allritz, M., Milfont, T. L., & Bilsky, W. (2015). Cross-cultural evidence of value structures and priorities in childhood. *British Journal of Psychology,* DOI:10.1111/bjop.12116.

Du, K. & Sim, N. (2016). Mergers, acquisitions, and bank efficiency: Cross-country evidence from emerging markets. *Research in International Business and Finance,* 36, 499–510.

Dundon, E. (2002). *The seeds of innovation: Cultivating the Synergy that Fosters New Ideas*. New York: AMACOM.

Durand, M. (2016). Employing critical incident technique as one way to display the hidden aspects of post-merger integration. *International Business Review*, 25, 87-102.

Dutordoir, M., Roosenboom, P., & Vasconcelos, M. (2014). Synergy disclosures in mergers and acquisitions. *International Review of Financial Analysis*, 31, 88-100.

Ellis, K. M., Lamont, B. T., Reus, T. H., & Faifman, L. (2015). Mergers and Acquisitions in Africa: A Review and an Emerging Research Agenda. *Africa Journal of Management*, 1(2), 137-171.

Ernst & Young (n.d.). *Capital Confidence Barometer*. Retrieved from http://www.ey.com/GL/en/Services/Transactions/EY-capital-confide nce-barometer.

Ernst & Young (2015). *Deal values soar to record highs as markets continue to reward deal making*. Retrieved from http://www.ey.com/US/en/ Newsroom/News-releases/news-deal-values-soar-to-record-highs-as-markets-continue-to-reward-deal making-says-EY.

FactSet (n.d.). *Flashwire Europe Quarterly*. Retrieved from http://www.factset.com/mergerstat_em/europe/Europe_Flashwire_Qua rterly.pdf.

Ferdman, B. M. (n.d.). The Practice of Inclusion in Diverse Organizations Toward a Systemic and Inclusive Framework. *Diversity at Work: The Practice of Inclusion.*

Firk, S., Maybuechen, F., Oehmichen, J., & Wolff, M. (2018). Value-based Management and Merger & Acquisition Returns: A Multi-level Contingency Model. *European Accounting Review*, 1-32. doi:10.1080/ 09638180.2018.1492947.

Galpin, T. J. & Herndon, M. (2014). *The Complete Guide to Mergers and Acquisitions Process Tools to Support M&A Integration at Every Level*. San Francisco, CA: Jossey-Bass.

Galpin, T. (2018). Reap exceptional value from M&A: Manage it as a core competence. *Strategy & Leadership, 46*(5), 17-25. doi: 10.1108/sl-05-2018-0054.

Garzella, S. & Fiorentino, R.(2014). A synergy measurement model to support the pre-deal decision making in mergers and acquisitions. *Management Decision*, 52(6), 1194 – 1216.

Geluebcke, J. P. W. (2015). The impact of foreign takeovers: comparative evidence from foreign and domestic acquisitions in Germany. *Applied Economics*, 47(8), 739-755.

Gertsen, M., Soederberg, A. M., & Vaara, E. (2004). *Cultural Change Processes in Mergers A social constructionist perspective*. Retrieved from http://openarchive.cbs.dk/bitstream/handle/10398/6942/wp38.pdf?sequence=1.

Gesteland, R. (2012). *Cross-Cultural Business Behavior A Guide for Global Management*. Denmark: Copenhagen Business School Press.

Golesorkhi, S., Mersland, R., Randøy, T., & Shenkar, O. (2019). The Performance Impact of Culture and Formal Institutional Differences in Cross-Border Alliances: The case of the Microfinance Industry. *International Business Review,* 28(1), 104-118. https://doi.org/10.1016/j.ibusrev.2018.08.006.

Golman, J. (2018, November 25). 5 largest failed M&A transactions of 2014. *Forbes*. Retrieved from http://www.forbes.com.

Gomes, E., Angwin, D., Peter, E., & Mellahi, K. (2012). HRM issues and outcomes in African mergers and acquisitions: a study of the Nigerian banking sector. *The International Journal of Human Resource Management*, 23(14), 2874-2900.

Gomes, E., Angwin, D. N., Weber, Y., & Tarba, S. Y. (2013). Critical Success Factors through the Mergers and Acquisitions Process: Revealing Pre- and Post-M&A Connections for Improved Performance. *Thunderbird International Business Review*, 55(1), 13–35.

Gomes, E., et al. (2014). A 22 year review of strategic alliance research in the leading management journals. *International Business Review*, http://dx.doi.org/10.1016/j.ibusrev.2014.03.005.

Gomes, E., Barnes, B.R., & Mahmood, T. (2016). A 22 year review of strategic alliance research in the leading management journals. *International Business Review,* 25, 15–27.

Gouveia, V. V., Vione, K. C., Milfont, T. L., & Fischer, R. (2015). Patterns of Value Change During the Life Span: Some Evidence From a Functional Approach to Values. *Personality and Social Psychology Bulletin*, 41(9), 1276-1290.

Hajro, A. (2014). Cultural influences and the mediating role of sociocultural integration processes on the performance of cross-border mergers and acquisitions. *The International Journal of Human Resource Management*, DOI: 10.1080/09585192.2014.922354.

Hajro, A. (2015). Cultural influences and the mediating role of socio-cultural integration processes on the performance of cross-border mergers and acquisitions. *The International Journal of Human Resource Management*, 26(2), 192-215.

Hanges, P. J., Aiken, J. R., Park, J., & Su, J. (2016). Cross-cultural leadership: leading around the world. *Current Opinion in Psychology*, 8, 64–69.

Harris, P. (2004). European leadership in cultural synergy. *European Business Review*, 16(4), 358-380.

Harrison, J. S., Hitt, M. A., & Ireland, R. D. (1991). Synergies and Post-Acquisition Performance: Differences versus Similarities in Resource Allocations. *Journal of Management*, 17(1), 173-190.

Hassan, I., Chidlow, A., & Romero-Martinez, A. M. (2016). Selection, valuation and performance assessment: Are these truly inter-linked within the M&A transactions. *International Business Review*, 25, 255–266.

Hassett, M. E., Reynolds, N., & Sandberg, B. (2018). The emotions of top managers and key persons in cross-border M&As: Evidence from a longitudinal case study. *International Business Review*, 27(4), 737-754. doi:10.1016/j.ibusrev.2017.12.003.

Harikkala-Laihinen, R., Hassett, M., Raitis, J., & Nummela, N. (2018). Dialogue as a source of positive emotions during cross-border post-acquisition socio-cultural integration. *Cross Cultural & Strategic Management, 25*(1), 183-208. doi:10.1108/ccsm-09-2016-0163.

He, Y. (2009). *Post-Acquisition Management in China*. Cambridge, UK: Chandos Publishing.

Hitt, M., King, D., Krishnan, H., Makri, M., & Schijven,M. (2009). Mergers and Acquisitions: Overcoming Pitfalls, Building Synergy, and Creating Value. *Business Horizons*, 52(6), 1-15.

Hitt, M. & Pisano, V. (2003). The Cross-Border Merger and Acquisition Strategy: A Research Perspective. *Management Research: The Journal of the Iberoamerican Academy of Management*, 1(2), 133 – 144.

Hofstede, G., Hofstede, G. J., & Minkov, M. (2010). *Cultures and Organizations: Software of the Mind, Intercultural Cooperation and Its Importance for Survival.* New York, NY: McGraw-Hill.

Huyghebaert, N. & Luypaert, M. (2013). Sources of Synergy Realization in Mergers and Acquisitions Empirical Evidence from Non-Serial Acquirers in Europe. *International Journal of Financial Research,* 4(2), 49-67.

Ismail, A. (2011). Does the Management's Forecast of Merger Synergies Explain the Premium Paid, the Method of Payment, and Merger Motives. *Financial Management*, 879-910.

Johannes, M. D. (n.d.). (Dis)Aggregating Alliance, Joint Venture, and Merger and Acquisition Performance: A Meta-Analysis. [Electronic version] *Advances in Mergers and Acquisitions,* 1-24.

Kang, H., Woo, W., Burton, R. M., & Mitchell, W. (2018). Constructing M&A valuation: How do merger evaluation methods differ as uncertainty and controversy vary? *Journal of Organization Design, 7*(1). doi:10.1186/s41469-017-0025-y.

Kim, J., Haleblian, J., & Finkelstein, S. (2011). When Firms Are Desperate to Grow via Acquisition: The Effect of Growth Patterns and Acquisition Experience on Acquisition Premiums. *Administrative Science Quarterly*, 56, 26–60.

King, D. R., Bauer, F., & Schriber, S. (2019). *Mergers and acquisitions a research overview*. London: Routledge.

Kling, G., Ghobadian, A., Hitt, M. A., Weitzel, U., & O'Regan, N. (2014). The Effects of Cross-border and Cross-industry Mergers and Acquisitions on Home-region and Global Multinational Enterprises. *British Journal of Management*, 25, S116–S132.

Klitmøller, A., Schneider, S. C., & Jonsen, K. (2015). Speaking of global virtual teams: language differences, social categorization and media choice. *Personnel Review*, 44(2), 270 – 285.

Knoll, S. (2008). *Cross-Business Synergies A Typology of Cross-Business Synergies and a Mid-Range Theory of Continuous Growth Synergy Realization*. Germany: Gabler-Verlag.

Kroon, D. P., Cornelissen, J. P., & Vaara, E. (2016). Explaining Employees' Reactions towards a Cross-Border Merger: The Role of English Language Fluency. *Manag Int Rev*, DOI: 10.1007/s11575-015-0259-2.

Larsson, R. & Finkelstein, S. (1999). Integrating Strategic, Organizational, and Human Resource Perspectives on Mergers and Acquisitions: A Case Survey of Synergy Realization. *Organization Science*, 10(1), 1-26.

Li Destri, A. M., Picone, P. M., & Mina, A. (2012). From "Strategic Fit" to Synergy Evaluation in M&A Deals. *Caspian Journal of Applied Sciences Research*, 1(12), 25-38.

Liu, Y. & Almor, T. (2016). How culture influences the way entrepreneurs deal with uncertainty in inter-organizational relationships: The case of returnee versus local entrepreneurs in China. *International Business Review*, 25, 4–14.

Lu, Q., Huang, X., & Bond, M. H. (2016). Culture and the Working Life: Predicting the Relative Centrality of Work Across Life Domains for Employed Persons. *Journal of Cross-Cultural Psychology*, 47(2), 277 – 293.

Łupina-Wegener, A., Schneider, S. C., & van Dick, R. (2015). The Role of Outgroups in Constructing a Shared Identity: A Longitudinal Study of a Subsidiary Merger in Mexico. *Manag Int Rev*, DOI 10.1007/s11575-015-0247-6.

Manos, R., Drori, I., Shoham, A., & Aharonson, B. S. (2015). National culture and national savings: is there a link? *International Review of Applied Economics,* 29(4), 455-481.

Marks, M. L. & Mirvis, P. H. (2010). *Joining Forces Making One Plus One Equal Three in Mergers, Acquisitions, and Alliances*. Revised and Updated Second Edition. San Francisco, US: Jossey-Bass.

Marks, M. L. & Mirvis, P. H. (2011). Merge Ahead A Research Agenda to Increase Merger and Acquisition Success. *J Bus Psychol*, 26, 161–168.

Marks, M. L. et al. (2014). Making the Most of Culture Clash in M&A. [Electronic version] *Leader to leader*, http://onlinelibrary.wiley.com/doi/10.1002/ltl.20113/pdf.

Meglio, O. (2009). Measuring Performance in Technology-Driven M&As: Insights From a Literature Review. *Advances in Mergers and Acquisitions*, 8, 103-118.

Meglio, O. & Risberg, A.(2011). The (mis)measurement of M&A performance–A systematic narrative literature review. *Scandinavian Journal of Management*, 27(4), 418-433.

Meglio, O., King, D. R., & Risberg, A. (2015). Improving Acquisition Outcomes with Contextual Ambidexterity. *Human Resource Management*, DOI:10.1002/hrm.21721.

Meier, O. & Schier, G. (2009). *Fusions, acquisitions, stratégie, finance, management*. France: Dunod.

Minkov, M., Bond, M.H., & Blagoev, V. (2015). Do different national samples yield similar dimensions of national culture? *Cross Cultural Management*, 22(2), 259 – 277.

Mirc, N. (2012). Connecting the micro- and macro-level: Proposition of a research design to study post-acquisition synergies through a social network approach. *Scandinavian Journal of Management,* 28, 121—135.

Nair, S. R., Demirbag, M., & Mellahi, K. (2015). Reverse Knowledge Transfer from Overseas Acquisitions A Survey of Indian MNEs. *Manag Int Rev*, 55, 277–301. DOI 10.1007/s11575-015-0242-y.

Peltokorpi, V., Allen, D. G., & Froese, F. (2015). Organizational embeddedness, turnover intentions, and voluntary turnover: The moderating effects of employee demographic characteristics and value orientations. *Journal of Organizational Behavior*, 36, 292–312. DOI: 10.1002/job.1981.

Picone, P. M. & Dagnino, G. B. (2015). Revamping research on unrelated diversification strategy: perspectives, opportunities and challenges for future inquiry. *J Manag Gov*, DOI 10.1007/s10997-014-9305-x.

Pignataro, P. (2015). *Mergers, Acquisitions, Divestitures, and Other Restructurings A Practical Guide to Investment Banking and Private Equity*. US: Wiley.

Porzio, M. (2018, January 08). Looking Ahead: M&A Trends In 2016. *Forbes*. Retrieved from http://www.forbes.com.

Primack, D. (2018, January 5). 2014 was a huge year for M&A and private equity. *Fortune*. Retrieved from http://fortune.com.

Proft, C. (2014). *The Speed of Human and Task Integration in Mergers and Acquisitions Human Integration as Basis for Task Integration*. Wiesbaden: Springer Fachmedien.

Raddawi, R. (2015). *Intercultural Communication with Arabs Studies in Educational, Professional and Societal Contexts.* Singapore: Springer-Verlag.

Rao-Nicholson, R., Khan, Z., & Stokes, P. (2016). Making great minds think alike: Emerging market multinational firms' leadership effects on targets' employee psychological safety after cross-border mergers and acquisitions. *International Business Review*, 25, 103–113.

Rao-Nicholson, R., Salaber, J., & Cao, T. H. (2016). Long-term performance of mergers and acquisitions in ASEAN countries. *Research in International Business and Finance*, 36, 373–387.

Reus, T. (2012). A Knowledge-Based View of Mergers and Acquisitions Revisited: Absorptive Capacity and Combinative Capability. *Advances in Mergers and Acquisitions*, 11, 69–88.

Reus, T. H., Lamont, B. T., & Ellis, K. M. (2015). A Darker Side of Knowledge Transfer Following International Acquisitions. *Strategic Management Journal,* DOI: 10.1002/smj.2373.

Reynolds, N. S. & Teerikangas, S. (2016). The international experience in domestic mergers – Are purely domestic M&A a myth? *International Business Review*, 25, 42–50.

Richter, N. F., Hauff, S., Schlaegel, C., Gudergan, S., Ringle, C. M., & Gunkel, M. (2016). Using Cultural Archetypes in Cross-cultural Management Studies. *Journal of International Management*, 22, 63–83.

Rkibi, T. (2009). Cunoaşterea Distanţelor Culturale Generează Avantaj Concurenţial? *Management intercultural*, XI(19), 2-38.

Roberts, H. (2018, January 6). Top 15 M&A deals of 2014. *Growth business*. Retrieved from http://www.growthbusiness.co.uk.

Rongxing, G. (2012). *Introduction to Intercultural Economics*. NY: Springer.

Rosinski, P. (2003). *Coaching Across Cultures-New Tools for Leveraging National, Corporate, and Professional Differences*. London: Nicholas Brealey Publishing.

Rothlauf, J. (2011). *Intercultural Leadership and Teams, BMS 3-rd Semester, 16 September 2011: Intercultural Aspects of Mergers and Acquisitions.* Retrieved from http://www.lscoop.com/files/CMS/Studie_M_A___FH-Stralsund.pdf.

Rottig, D. (2013). A Marriage Metaphor Model for Sociocultural Integration in International Mergers and Acquisitions. *Thunderbird International Business Review*, 55(4), 439-451.

Sahoo, P., Nataraj, G., & Dash R. K. (2014). *Foreign Direct Investment in South Asia Policy, Impact, Determinants and Challenges*. India: Springer.

Sarala, R. M., Junni, P., Cooper, C. L., & Tarba, S. Y. (2014). A Sociocultural Perspective on Knowledge Transfer in Mergers and Acquisitions. *Journal of Management*, XX(X), 1–20.

Sarala, R. M., Vaara, E., & Junni, P. (2017). Beyond merger syndrome and cultural differences: New avenues for research on the "human side" of global mergers and acquisitions (M&As). *Journal of World Business*. doi:10.1016/j.jwb.2017.10.001.

Sinha, P., Daellenbach, U., & Bednarek, R. (2015). Legitimacy defense during post-merger integration: Between coupling and compartmentalization. *Strategic Organization*, 13(3), 169–199.

Schumacker, R. E. & Lomax, R. G. (2010). *A beginner's guide to structural equation modelling*, Third Edition. US: Routledge.

Schwartz, S. H. (2012). An Overview of the Schwartz Theory of Basic Values. *Online Readings in Psychology and Culture*, 2(1). http://dx.doi.org/10.9707/2307-0919.1116.

Schwerdtfeger, M. (2015, January 13). Will 2015 be another great year for M&A? *Forbes*. Retrieved from http://www.forbes.com.

Seo, M. & Hill, N. S. (2005). Understanding the Human Side of Merger and Acquisition: An Integrative Framework. *The Journal of Applied Behavioral Science*, 41(4), 422-443.

Shenkar, O. (2012). Cultural distance revisited: Towards a more rigorous conceptualization and measurement of cultural differences. *Journal of International Business Studies*, 43, 1-11.

Sonenshine, R. & Reynolds, K. (2014). Determinants of cross-border merger premia', *Rev World Econ*, 150, 173-189.

Stahl, K. S., Angwin, D. N., Very, P., Gomes, E., Weber, Y., Tarba, S. Y., Noorderhaven, N., Benyamini, H., Bouckenooghe, D., Chreim, S., Durand, M., Hassett, M. E., Kokk, G., Mendenhall, M. E., Mirc, N., Miska, C., Park, K. M., Reynolds, N. S., Rouzies, A., Sarala, R. M., Seloti, S. L., Søndergaard, M., & Yildiz, H. E. (2013). Sociocultural Integration in Mergers and Acquisitions: Unresolved Paradoxes and Directions for Future Research. *Thunderbird International Business Review*, 55(4), 333–356.

Stahl, G. K. & Voigt, A. (2005). Impact of Cultural Differences on Merger and Acquisition Performance: A Critical Research Review and An Integrative Model. *Advances in Mergers and Acquisitions*, 4, 51–82.

Stiles, P., Trevor, J., Farndale, E., Morris, S. S., Paauwe, J., Stahl, G. K., & Wright, P. (2015). Changing Routine: Reframing Performance Management within a Multinational. *Journal of Management Studies,* 52(1). DOI: 10.1111/joms.12111

Straub, T. (2007). *Reasons for Frequent Failure in Mergers and Acquisitions*. Wiesbaden: Deutscher Universitäts-Verlag.

Street Insider (n.d). *2014's Top Deals*. Retrieved from http://www.streetinsider.com/ma_top_deals.php?year=2014

Street Insider *(n.d). 2015's Top U.S. Takeover Deals.* Retrieved from http://www.streetinsider.com/ma_top_deals.php?year=2015.

Teerikangas, S., & Laamanen, T.(n.d.). Structure First! Temporal Dynamics of Structural and Cultural Integration in Cross-Border Acquisitions. [Electronic version]Advances in Mergers and Acquisitions, 109-152.

Teerikangas, S. & Very, P. (2012). Culture in mergers and acquisitions: a critical synthesis and steps forward. In D. Faulkner, S. Teerikangas, J. J.

Joseph (Eds), *The Handbook of Mergers and Acquisitions* (pp.392-430). Oxford: Oxford University Press.

Teerikangas, S., Véry, P., & Pisano, V. (2011). Integration Managers' Value-Capturing Roles and Acquisition Performance. *Human Resource Management*, 50(5), 651 –683.

Teerikangas, S., & Thanos, I. (2017). Looking into the 'black box': unlocking the effect of integration on acquisition performance. *European Management Journal.* doi:10.1016/j.emj.2017.06.002.

Teerikangas, S., & Reynolds, N. (2018). Chapter 1 Reflecting on the Use of Ethnographic Methods in the Study of Mergers. *Advances in Mergers and Acquisitions,* 1-29. doi:10.1108/s1479-361x20180000017001.

Thomson Reuters (n.d.). *Full Year 2014 | Mergers & Acquisitions | Financial Advisors*. Retrieved from http://dmi.thomsonreuters.com/Content/Files/4Q2014_Global_MandA_Legal_Advisory_Review.pdf

Thomson Reuters. (2017). *Mergers & Acquisitions Review Full Year 2016*. Retrieved from http://share.thomson reuters.com/general/PR/MA_4Q_2016_E.pdf.

Thomson reuters. (2018). *Mergers & Acquisitions Review Full Year 2017*. Retrieved from https://www.thomsonreuters.co.jp/content/dam/openweb/documents/pdf/japan/market-review/2017/ma-4q-2017-e.pdf.

Thomson Reuters. (2019). *Mergers & Acquisitions Review Full Year 2018*. Retrieved from http://dmi.thomsonreuters. com/Content/Files/4Q2018_MNA_Financial_Advisory_Review.pdf.

Travers, F. J. (2004). *Investment Manager Analysis: A Comprehensive Guide to Portfolio Selection, Monitoring and Optimization*. Hoboken, New Jersey: Wiley.

Trompenaars, F. & Asser, MN (2010). *The Global M and A Tango: Cross-cultural Dimensions of Mergers and Acquisitions.* New York: McGraw-Hill.

Ulijn, J., Duysters, G., & Meijer,E. (2010). *Strategic Alliances, Mergers and Acquisitions: The Influence of Culture on Successful Cooperation*. Cheltenham: Edward Elgar Publishing.

Vaara, E., Junni, P., Sarala, R., Ehrnrooth, M., & Koveshnikov, A. (2013). Attributional Tendencies in Cultural Explanations of M&A Performance. *Strategic Management Journal*, 1-33.

Van Marrewijk, A. (2016). Conflicting subcultures in mergers and acquisitions: a longitudinal study of integrating a radical internet firm into a bureaucratic telecoms firm. *British Journal of Management*, 00, 1–17.

Vauclair, C. M., Fischer, R., Ferreira, M. C., Guerra, V., Hößler, U., Karabati, S., de Carvalho Filho, M. K., Porto, J. B., Reyes, M. L., Rytkönen, J., & Spieß, E. (2015). What Kinds of Value Motives Guide People in Their Moral Attitudes? The Role of Personal and Prescriptive Values at the Culture Level and Individual Level. *Journal of Cross-Cultural Psychology*, 46(2), 211–228.

Veiss, S. D. & Abrudan, I. (2012). Experimental studies based on the model of Hofstede. *Acta Technica Napocensis Series: Applied Mathematics and Mechanics*, 55, 939-948.

Very, P., Metais, E., Lo, S., & Hourquet, P. G. (2012). Can We Predict M&A Activity? *Advances in Mergers and Acquisitions*, 11, 1–32.

Viegas-Pires, M. (2013). Multiple Levels of Culture and Post M&A Integration: A Suggested Theoretical Framework. *Thunderbird International Business Review*, 55(4), 357-370.

Vinzi, V. E., Chin, W. W., Henseler, J., & Wang, H. (2010). *Handbook of Partial Least Squares Concepts, Methods and Applications*. Germany: Springer-Verlag.

Warter, I. & Warter, L. (2014a). Latest Trends in Mergers and Acquisitions Research. The New Pattern of Globalization. *Bulletin of The Polytechnic Institute of Iasi*, LX (LXIV)(2), 25-43.

Warter, L. & Warter, I. (2014b). Intercultural Issues in Mergers and Acquisitions. Are Cultural Differences an Asset or a Liability? *Bulletin of The Polytechnic Institute of Iasi*, LX (LXIV)(2), 9-24.

Warter, L. & Warter, I. (2015a). Cultural Due Diligence as Competitive Advantage in Cross-Border Mergers and Acquisitions. *Bulletin of The Polytechnic Institute of Iasi*, LXI (LXV)(1), 59-72.

Warter, I. & Warter, L. (2015b). Intercultural Negotiation in Mergers Andacquisitions. The Integration of The Cultural Dimension into The Negotiation Domain. *Bulletin of The Polytechnic Institute of Iasi*, LXI (LXV)(1), 73-86.

Warter, I. & Warter, L. (2015c). The new face of global M&A. Intercultural issues in banking industry. *Forum Scientiae Oeconomia*, 3(1), 127-138.

Warter, L. & Warter, I. (2015d). A M&A process perspective in the banking sector. *Forum Scientiae Oeconomia*, 3(2), 105-115.

Warter, I. & Warter, L. (2015e). Implications of M&As For Banking Industry. From Cultural Fit To Cultural Clashes. In A. Roman, S. G. Anton & I. Bilan (Eds), *Euro and the European banking system: evolutions and challenges* (pp. 367-376). Iasi: Editura Universitatii "Alexandru Ioan Cuza.

Warter, L. & Warter, I. (2015f). Can Mergers And Acquisitions Improve Banking Industry? In A. Roman, S. G. Anton & I. Bilan (Eds), *Euro and the European banking system: evolutions and challenges* (pp. 377-386). Iasi: Editura Universitatii "Alexandru Ioan Cuza.

Warter, I. & Warter, L. (2015g). A pluralistic perspective on intercultural decision-making in M&As. *Forum Scientiae Oeconomia*, 3(4), 25-36.

Warter, L. & Warter, I. (2017a). Organizational Functions and Core Values: Intercultural Matters. In A. Jabłoński (Ed), *Sustainability and Scalability of Business: Theory and Practice* (pp. 97-112). NY: Nova Science Publishers.

Warter, I. & Warter, L. (2017b). Responsibility, Strategy and Business Value: Intercultural Approach to Strategic Management. In A. Jabłoński (Ed), *Sustainability and Scalability of Business: Theory and Practice* (pp. 113-133). NY: Nova Science Publishers.

Warter, L. & Warter, I. (2018a). Company's culture before M&A. A new evaluation framework for managers' perception. In K. Szczepańska-Woszczyna & Z. Dacko-Pikiewicz (Eds), *Innovation processes in the social space of the organization* (pp. 287-308). NY: Nova Science Publishers.

Warter, I. & Warter, L. (2018b). Negotiation in M&A. Culture: the hidden factor for success. In K. Szczepańska-Woszczyna & Z. Dacko-

Pikiewicz (Eds), *Innovation processes in the social space of the organization* (pp. 261-285). NY: Nova Science Publishers.

Weber, Y. & Drori, I. (2011). Integrating Organizational and Human Behavior Perspectives on Mergers and Acquisitions Looking Inside the Black Box. *Int. Studies of Mgt. & Org*, 41(3), 76-95.

Weber, Y., Drori, I., & Tarba, S. Y. (2012). Culture-performance relationships in mergers and acquisition: the role of trust. *European J. Cross-Cultural Competence and Management*, 2(3/4),252–274.

Weber, Y., Rachman-Moore, D., & Tarba, S. Y. (2012). HR practices during post-merger conflict and merger performance. *International Journal of Cross Cultural Management*, 12(1), 73-99.

Weber, Y. & Tarba, S. Y. (2013). Sociocultural Integration in Mergers and Acquisitions—New Perspectives. *Thunderbird International Business Review*, 55(4), 327-331.

Weber, Y., Tarba, S., & Reichel, A. (2009). International Mergers and Acquisitions Performance Revisited –The Role of Cultural Distance and Post-Acquisition Integration Approach. *Advances in Mergers and Acquisitions*, 8, 1–17.

Weber, Y., Tarba, S., & Reichel, A. (2011). A Model of the Influence of Culture on Integration Approaches and International Mergers and Acquisitions Performance. *Int. Studies of Mgt. & Org,* 41(3), 9-24.

Weber, Y., Tarba, S. Y., & Rozen Bachar, Z. (2011). Mergers and acquisitions performance paradox: the mediating role of integration approach. *European J. International Management*, 5(4), 373–393.

Weber, Y., Tarba, S. Y., & Rozen Bachar, Z. (2012). The effects of culture clash on international mergers in the high tech industry. *World Review of Entrepreneurship, Management and Sustainable Development*, 8(1), 103–118.

Whitaker, S. C. (2012). *Mergers & Acquisitions Integration Handbook: Helping Companies Realize The Full Value of Acquisitions*. Hoboken, New Jersey: John Wiley & Sons.

Wursten, H. (n.d.a). Culture and Change Management. Geert Hofstede. Retrieved from https://geert-hofstede.com/tl_files/Culture%20and%20Change%20Management%20huib.pdf.

Wursten, H. (n.d.b). *Mental images The influence of culture on (economic) policy*. UNPAN. Retrieved from http://unpan1.un.org/intradoc/groups/public/documents/un/unpan002455.pdf.

Wursten, H. (2017). *Mental images of culture, a perspective to understand misunderstandings in politics, business, religion* & Retrieved from https://www.academia.edu/34319656/Mental_images_of_culture_a_perspective_to_understand_misunderstandings_in_politics_business_religion_and_.

Wursten, H. & Lanzer, F. (n.d.). *The EU: the third European cultural contribution to the world*. Club of Amsterdam. Retrieved from http://www.clubofamsterdam.com/contentarticles/86%20Europe/itim%20eu%20report.pdf.

Xing, Y., et al. (2014). Intercultural influences on managing African employees of Chinese firms in Africa: Chinese managers' HRM practices. *International Business Review*, http://dx.doi.org/10.1016/j.ibusrev.2014.05.003.

Xing, Y., Liu, Y.,Tarba, S.Y., & Cooper, C.L. (2016). Intercultural influences on managing African employees of Chinese firms in Africa: Chinese managers' HRM practices. *International Business Review*, 25, 28–41.

Yildiz, H. E. (2014). Not All Differences Are the Same: Dual Roles of Status and Cultural Distance in Sociocultural Integration in Cross-border M&As. *Journal of International Management*, 20, 25-37.

Yildiz, H. E. (2016). "Us vs. them" or "us over them" On the roles of similarity and status in M&As. *International Business Review*, 25, 51–65.

Younge, K. A., Tong, T. W., & Fleming, L. (2015). How Anticipated Employee Mobility Affects Acquisition Likelihood Evidence from a Natural Experiment. *Strategic Management Journal,* 36, 686–708.

Zaheer, A., Castañer, X., & Souder, D. (2013). Synergy Sources, Target Autonomy, and Integration in Acquisitions. *Journal of Management*, 39(3), 604-632.

Zaidman, N. (2001). Cultural Codes and Language Strategies in Business Communication: Interactions between Israeli and Indian

Businesspeople. *Management Communication Quarterly*, 14(3), 408-441.

Zait, D., Warter, L., & Warter, I. (2014). Cross-Cultural Incentives for the FDI. *Cross-Cultural Management Journal*, XVI(1(30)), 798-811.

Zander, U. & Zander, L. (2010). Opening the grey box: Social communities, knowledge and culture in acquisitions. *Journal of International Business Studies*, 21, 27-37.

Zhang, J., Ahammad, M. F., Tarba, S., Cooper, C. L., Glaister, K. W., & Wang, J. (2014). The effect of leadership style on talent retention during Merger and Acquisition integration: evidence from China. *The International Journal of Human Resource Management*, DOI: 10.1080/09585192.2014.908316.

Zhang, J., Ahammad, M. F., Tarba, S., Cooper, C. L., Glaister, K. W., & Wang, J. (2015). The effect of leadership style on talent retention during Merger and Acquisition integration: evidence from China. *The International Journal of Human Resource Management*, 26(7), 1021-1050.

About the Author

Liviu Warter is Founder & Vice President of the Center for Socio-Economic Studies and Multiculturalism in Iasi, Romania (http://csesm.warter.ro/). He is Editor of Journal of Intercultural Management and Ethics (http://jime.warter.ro/)

He is a consultant specialized in acquisition/merger/restructuring processes and strategic planning. He is Partner of Consulting Experts-Warter from Iasi, Romania (http://www.warter.ro), a company specialized in providing management, mergers, acquisitions and investments consulting.

He speaks fluent English, French, Hebrew and Romanian.

He published book chapters and scientific articles on intercultural management, foreign direct investments, cross border M&A, intercultural synergy, intercultural due diligence, strategic management, innovation, business ethics, Jewish business ethics, Holocaust studies (https://www.researchgate.net/profile/Liviu_Warter).

He holds a PhD in Intercultural Management, a M. A. in Management and a MSc. Degree in Mechanical Engineering.

INDEX

A

B

C

J

L

M

N

O

P

Q

R

S

T

U

V

Related Nova Publications

Trust Throughput Modeling Pathways

Author: Waymond Rodgers

Series: Ethical Issues in the 21st Century

Book Description: The Throughput Modeling approach indicates how six different trust behaviors can be guided, how trust decision making can be improved and made defensible, and how special problems facing individuals, relational systems, and institutions can be dealt with via decision-making pathways leading to action.

Hardcover ISBN: 978-1-53615-191-6
Retail Price: $195

Small Business: Funding, Management and Mentor Programs

Editor: Angel Becker

Series: Business Issues, Competition and Entrepreneurship

Book Description: Congressional interest in small business access to capital has increased in recent years because of concerns that small businesses might be prevented from accessing sufficient capital to enable them to start, continue, or expand operations and create jobs.

Hardcover ISBN: 978-1-53615-969-1
Retail Price: $230

Related Nova Publications

Workplace Bullying in African Tertiary Institutions

Author: Ilongo Fritz Ngale

Series: Business Issues, Competition and Entrepreneurship

Book Description: *Workplace Bullying in African Tertiary Institutions* reveals the link between workplace bullying and on-going university restructuring programmes, in which the latter are portrayed as being executed through a pro-bullying neoliberalist ethos.

Hardcover ISBN: 978-1-53615-894-6
Retail Price: $160

Private Equity Globalisation: Ethical Business Challenges

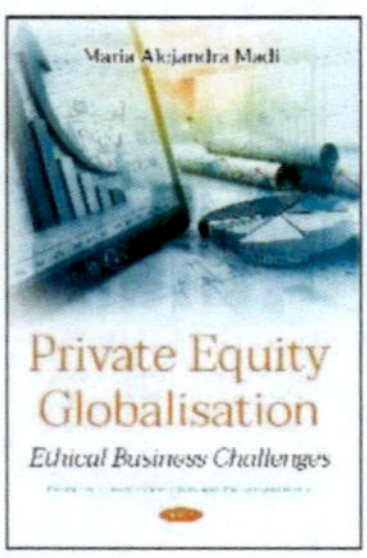

Author: Maria Alejandra Madi

Series: Business Issues, Competition and Entrepreneurship

Book Description: This book aims to fill a gap in existing literature in order to contribute to the understanding of the main features and outcomes of the private equity business model that has already been spread around the world. Private equity funds have been drivers of the financialisation of the global economy.

Softcover ISBN: 978-1-53615-043-8
Retail Price: $95

To see a complete list of Nova publications, please visit our website at www.novapublishers.com